For You!

MODERN DAY LOVE LETTERS

JOHN ARSENAULT

Daylight

Cofounders: Taj Forer and Michael Itkoff
Creative Director: Ursula Damm
Designer: Jonathan San Nicolas
Copy Editors: Nancy Hubbard, Barbara Richard

ISBN 978-1-942084-44-0

Printed by Artron, China

Daylight Books
E-mail: info@daylightbooks.org
Web: www.daylightbooks.org

DEDICATED TO

MY MOTHER, JUDY, AND MY FATHER, JOE, XX

FOR YOU! MODERN DAY LOVE LETTERS

I share an obsession of roses with my aunts Kathy and Meme, which has been passed down to us from their mother, my late grandmother Elizabeth. Our love for roses is a family tradition—but where the women in the family love floral printed wallpaper, I prefer to capture their beauty via photography. This is a way for me to honor my grandmother and my family roots.

My intention wasn't to show ideal beauty or perfection, but rather show beauty through the imperfections—the natural blemishes and bruises define their beauty. Contrasts between new growth and dying petals give the images a tactile quality. There's a darkness to these flowers even in the light of day—a mysteriousness and sensuality. My goal was to capture portraits of roses, celebrating the process of aging with an evocative, dreamlike quality; a nod to the twentieth-century painter Georgia O'Keeffe.

There's also an underlying intimacy in this body of work. Originally, I photographed the images as modern day love letters for my partner, Raf; I posted the images each time with a simple title *For You!* without describing or mentioning Raf because I wanted to keep our new relationship private. Slowly, these flowers have become a gift to everyone: For You!

In 2016, four years into photographing *For You!*, I began taking weekly still-life images of roses purchased from the local farmers market. Raf and I enjoyed the routine of walking to the market and choosing our flowers: I came to see the images as weekly portraits. *For You!* reinforces my love for the inherent appeal of youth, but also celebrates the beauty of aging.

Unfortunately, Raf was never able to meet my grandmother Elizabeth. I'll be forever grateful to both of them for inspiring *For You!*

John Arsenault
January 3, 2017
New York City

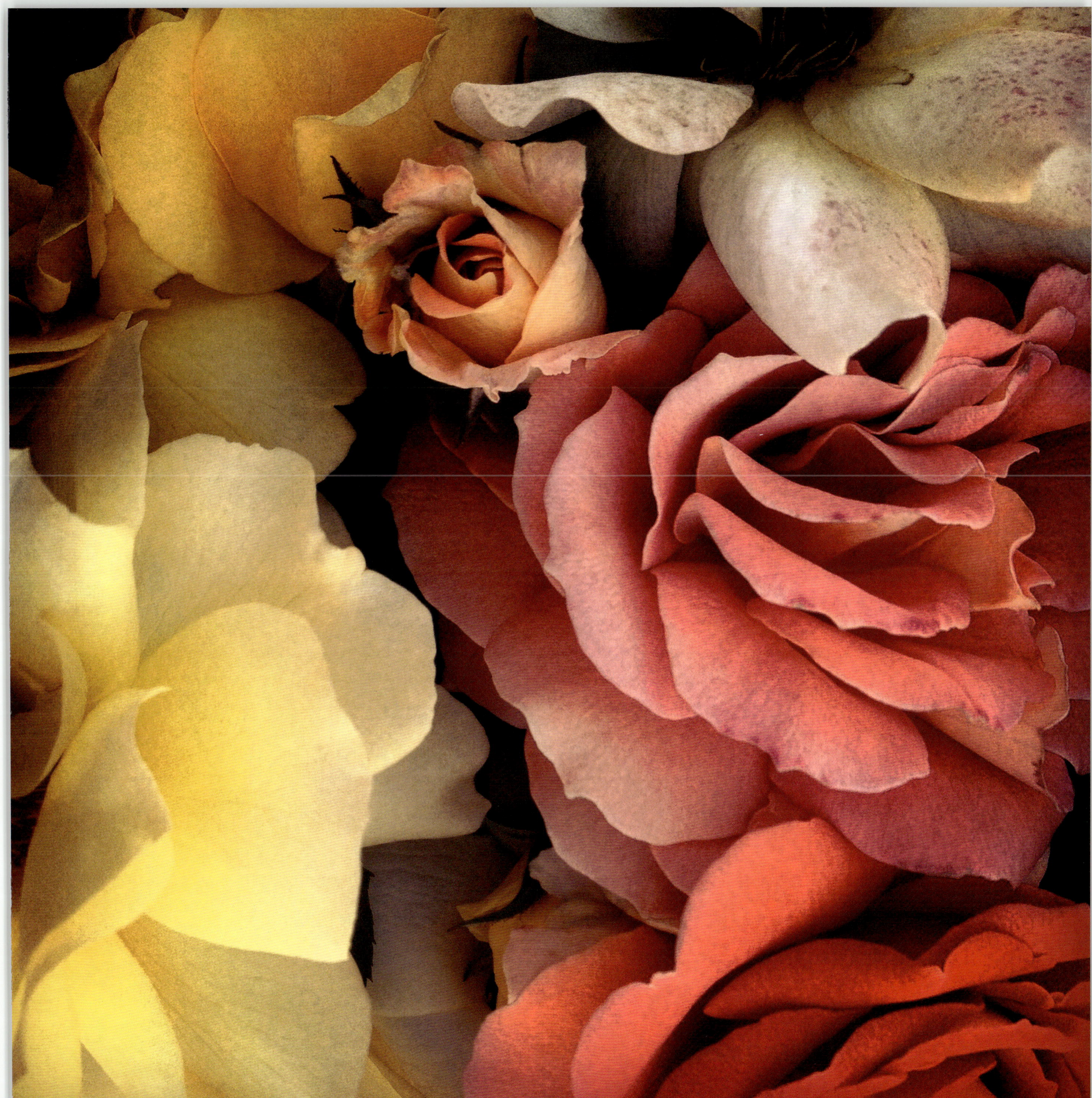

A SHARED TRIBUTE

Brian Paul Clamp

Singer and songwriter Morrissey has been quoted as dryly stating, “I think flowers are very beautiful things. Very nice and innocent things. They don’t harm anybody.”

Let’s now go back to June 15, 1991, when Steven Patrick Morrissey, then just thirty-two years old, burst onto the stage in Denver, Colorado, with flowers in his hands, flowers sprouting from his pockets, and even more flowers falling at his feet thrown from all parts of a screaming audience. I was one of those adoring fans—a twenty-one-year-old devotee, and this was my first opportunity to see Morrissey in the flesh. And the exuberant flower explosion was genuinely surprising, dare I say, even emotional.

Morrissey’s association with flowers likely goes back to his idol Oscar Wilde, who also adored them and is now famously remembered for the trademark green carnation he wore in his lapel (which has come to stand as a wearable symbol for declaring one’s homosexuality). Morrissey’s original band, The Smiths, filmed one of their two videos for their 1983 hit “This Charming Man” in a room filled wall-to-wall with nothing but flowers. In fact, critics of The Smiths pejoratively referred to the foursome as the “Flower Wimps.” Nonetheless, while surly crowds at other shows would hurl awful things at the stage, ranging from spit to bottles, Morrissey expressed love for his fans who instead would bring him fresh blooms, notably heaps and heaps of gladioli, the singer’s favorite.

All of this is not simply one dizzy queen’s sappy reverie. I mention Morrissey and his passion for flowers for several reasons. For one, John Arsenault, two years my junior, was also a certified Morrissey fanatic. In fact, many of the titles of the artist’s photographs over the years come directly from Morrissey’s legendary lyrics. *The Youngest Was the Most Loved, There Never Was a Woman of My Dreams, Heaven Knows I’m Miserable Now*—these are all in homage to the performer. But the titles are also what one might term “Piccadilly Palare.” (Morrissey sang about *polari*—a secret slang language first used by thieves and beggars in the nineteenth century and later taken up by male hustlers in London in the 1960s. By speaking polari, campy male prostitutes would know only others of their kind could decipher the meaning of their words, thus disguising certain sexual predilections illegal there until 1967.)

But “dizzy” is of import here, too, as it brings to mind Morrissey’s fey and flustered “Hairdresser on Fire” from 1988. Again, I promise this is not out of the blue, as John Arsenault actually studied styling at the renowned Vidal Sassoon Salon in Boston before deciding to move to New York, go back to school, and pursue photography at the School of Visual Arts.

Arsenault began shooting flowers here and there from the very beginning of his artistic career. Whether growing in a garden or arranged in a bouquet on a table, the quotidian subject matter was irresistible to him, and he has visited it again and again. However, it was not until years later, in 2013, after he moved from New York to Provincetown and then on to Los Angeles, that floral compositions would begin to comprise an independent body of work. Working a night job with which he was not always enamored, shooting flowers during the day was partly a means to lift his spirits and make his way back to photography professionally in a new city.

Indeed, much of John Arsenault's artwork is about being happy—unafraid to celebrate and enjoy simple beauty. *For You! Modern Day Love Letters* is a romantic and hopeful body of work. It reflects the artist's personality—his generosity and optimism; his ability to think positively about the future and all it may hold.

To conclude with a final nod to Morrissey and his original brand of poetry—just one of my many shared enthusiasms with the photographer whose work is the subject of this monograph: There is no harsh truth to Arsenault's camera eye.

FOR YOU!: JOHN ARSENAULT SUB ROSA

Rock Hushka

John Arsenault loves beauty.[1] That's his terrible secret. He turns his lens and critical eye toward people and places of his daily life and captures the kind of moments that most people overlook. In these elusive slips of time, Arsenault manages to capture grace and dignity. For more than twenty years, his photographs brought to the fore the special qualities of light, tattoos, taste, style, humor, desire, and, always, pathos. It is not surprising, then, to learn that he discovered the ecstatic beauty of roses.

The rose photographs of *For You! Modern Day Love Letters* make up part of the artist's larger body of work, which coalesce into a type of visual diary. Another includes *Barmaid* snapshots taken at the Eagle, a leather bar in Los Angeles, and another self-portraits.[2] The rose photographs are important in themselves because they provide the tenderest glimpse into the artist's practice.

The roses have become somewhat of a mild obsession for Arsenault. He will spot a rose bush or garden at any time during his daily routine in Los Angeles. Most often he'll catch a flicker of color out of the corner of his eye, then refocus his attention and begin to search for the elusive photograph of exquisite beauty. As he photographs, he composes for depth of field and color arrangements. He is searching for that virtually indescribable something to stir his emotions and provide authentic response to his pursuit of beauty.

The photographs in For You! initially began with images he made using only his iPhone, then uploaded to Instagram. Because of this nearly ubiquitous and fairly inexpensive technology, the impact of the photographs seems almost miraculous. For Arsenault, the iPhone and Instagram provide a newer, more interactive working method.[3]

He recently expanded the series by focusing on traditional still-life arrangements and photographing with a digital 35 mm camera. Arsenault subverted the typical conventions of still life by gathering the roses into plastic and glass containers of no particular beauty. Almost despite his careful efforts to emphasize the quiet and mundane, he captured the intensity of the soon-to-wither flowers. Their beauty pushes against every edge of the photographs.

The images in *For You!* harken back to a kind of beauty that once seemed almost sentimental and old-fashioned. It is worth commenting that roses as a subject are almost absurdly saccharine, the territory of natty gardeners and nineteenth-century artists. Arsenault manages to make roses edgy and toxically poignant. He suspends color and time within the photograph, allowing the viewer to indulge his or her need for aesthetic experience so intensely simple and so primordially integrated into the soul that any sense of shame fades into pure enjoyment.

Arsenault's images give a twenty-first century response to the Western tradition of symbolism of roses. American modernists such a Marsden Hartley (1877–1943) and Georgia O'Keeffe (1887–1986) found pure form and an unconscious expression of sexuality in the flowers. Artists in the nineteenth century, such as Pierre-Joseph Redouté (1759–1840), looked to the rose painting as a practice of scientific taxonomy and technical brilliance. Others such as Henri Fantin-Latour (1836–1904) sought to apply aspects of modernism to the still-life tradition refined by the Dutch flower painters of the seventeenth century. Looking at Arsenault's roses, it is difficult not to feel the tug of these divergent histories while layering his own feelings of fragility tinged with a darker aspect of impending decay and morbidity. The late blooms remind us that this is inevitable.

His tension of beauty of the foreboding makes his roses virtually unforgettable to the close observer. Arsenault is shamelessly sharing all kinds of secrets with us—about photography and the history of art, about beauty, about death, and about traditions unbroken since the days of ancient philosophers, artists, and priest-figures. Death unites us all.

The ancients believed the rose symbolized love and desire, and this remains unbroken for centuries: "The rose, the emblem of love, was given by Cupid as a bribe to Harpocrates, the god of silence, whence originated the custom in northern countries of suspending a rose from the ceiling at meetings where secrecy was enjoined. Carvings of roses are seen on the ceilings of old dining halls in this country and are probably the origin of the 'ceiling rose,' the ornamental centre-piece of the ceilings of most Victorian houses."[4] From these now obscure origins, we have the term *sub rosa*.

Arsenault keeps us under the spell of the rose. His photographs allow us into his confidence through the enchantment of beauty then to the sublime and, ultimately, to admission of the difficulties and pain of our time. Through his photographs, we've agreed to his logic and conclusions, and we share his secrets.

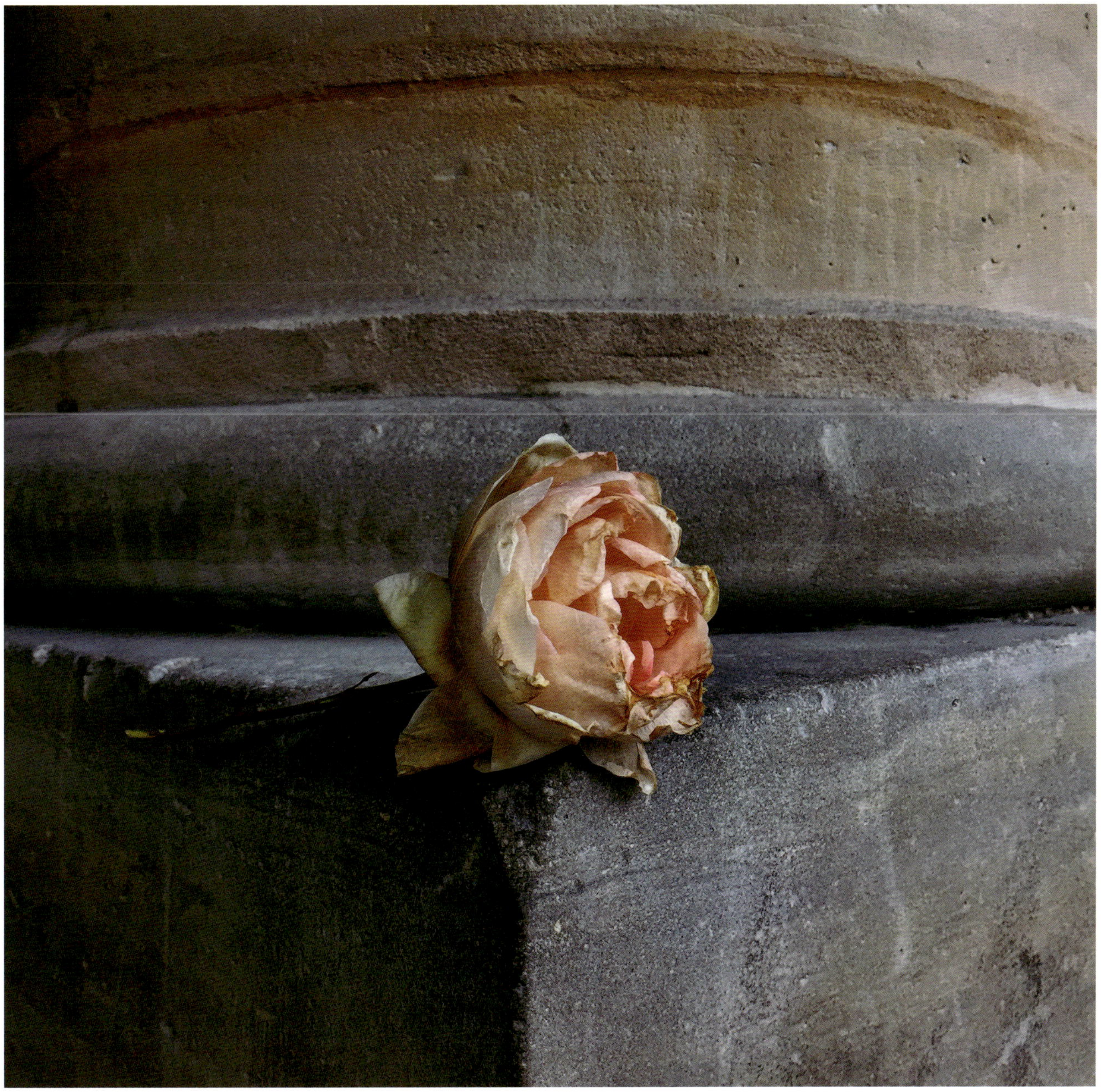

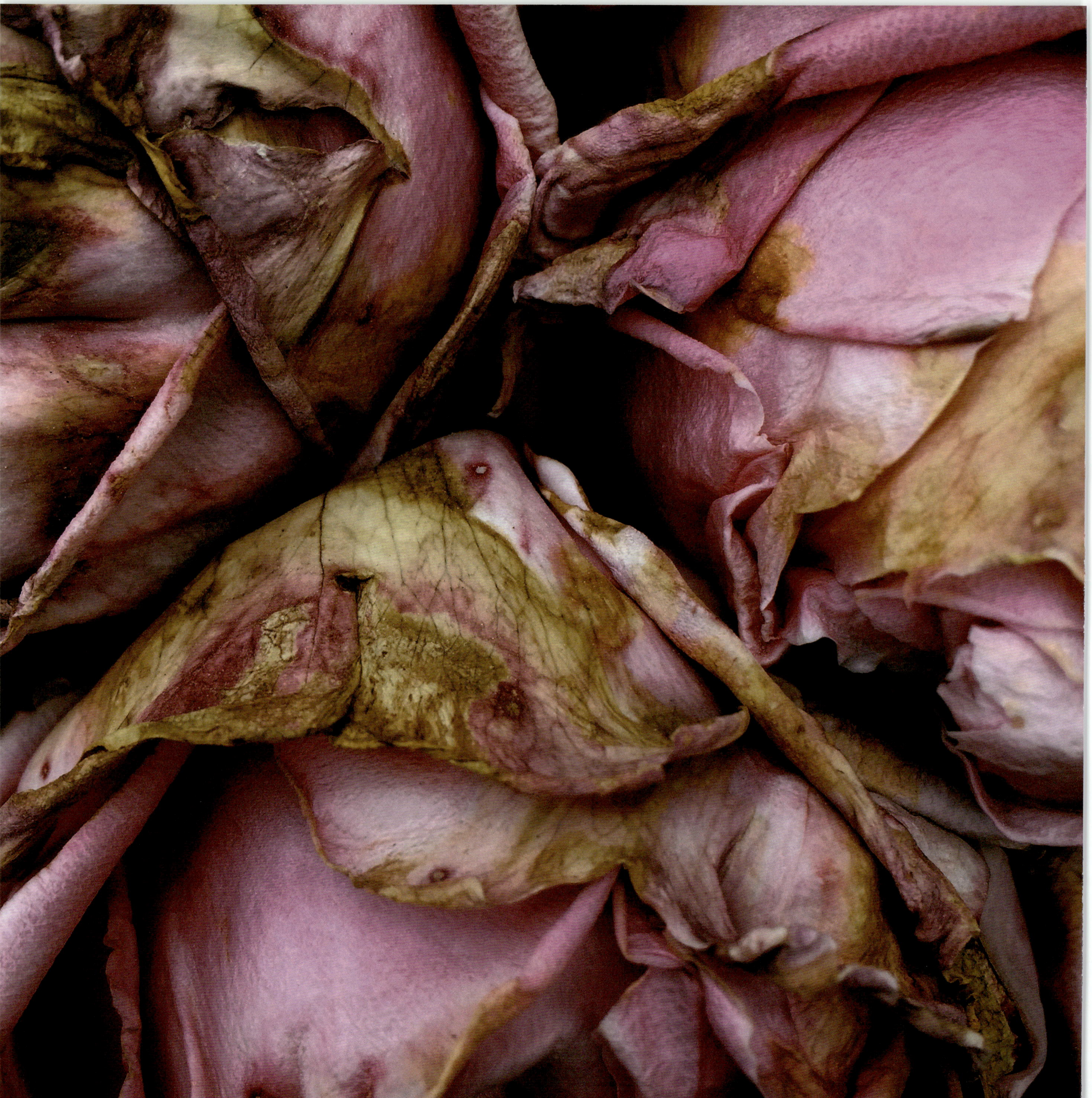

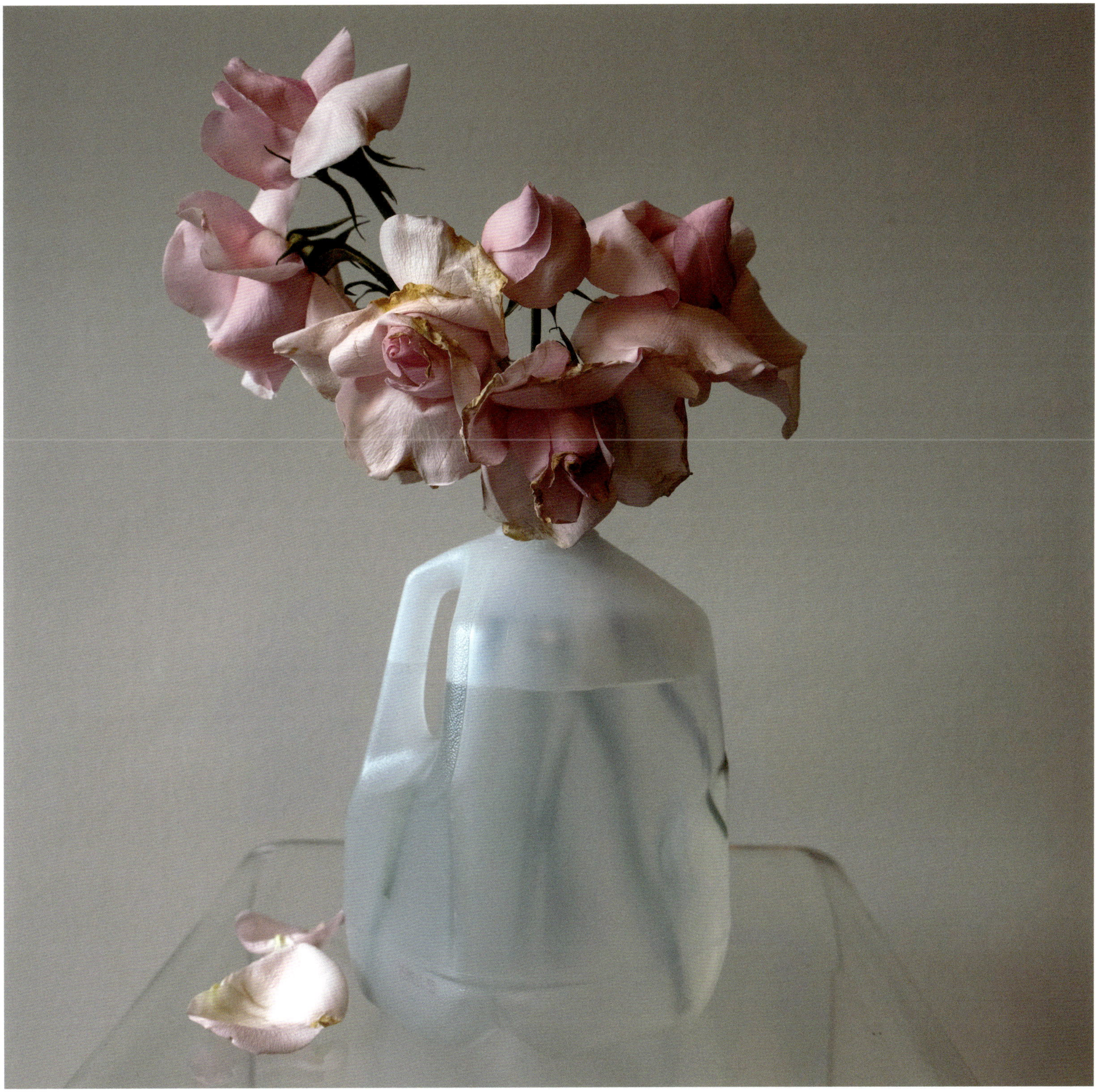

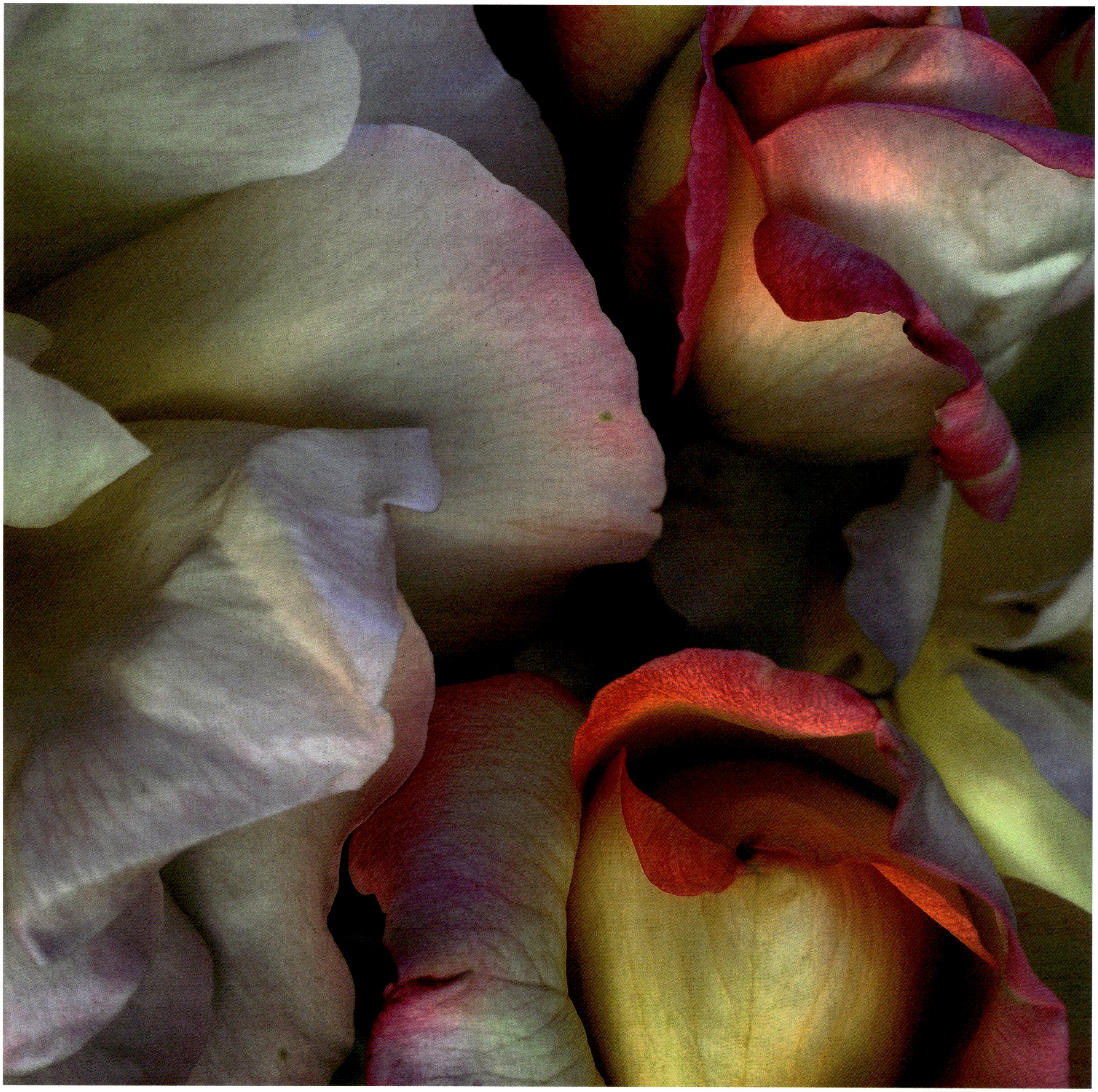

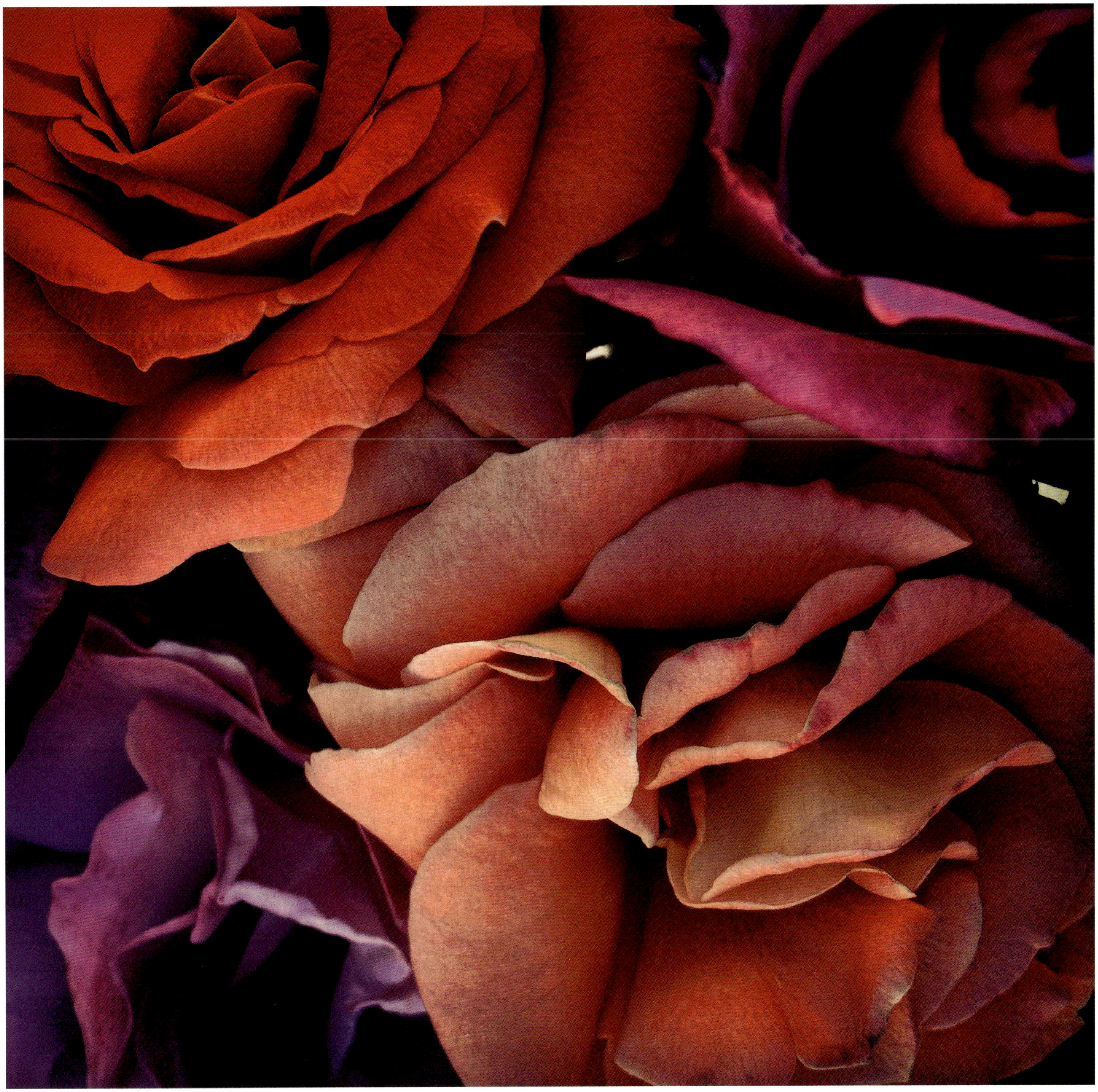

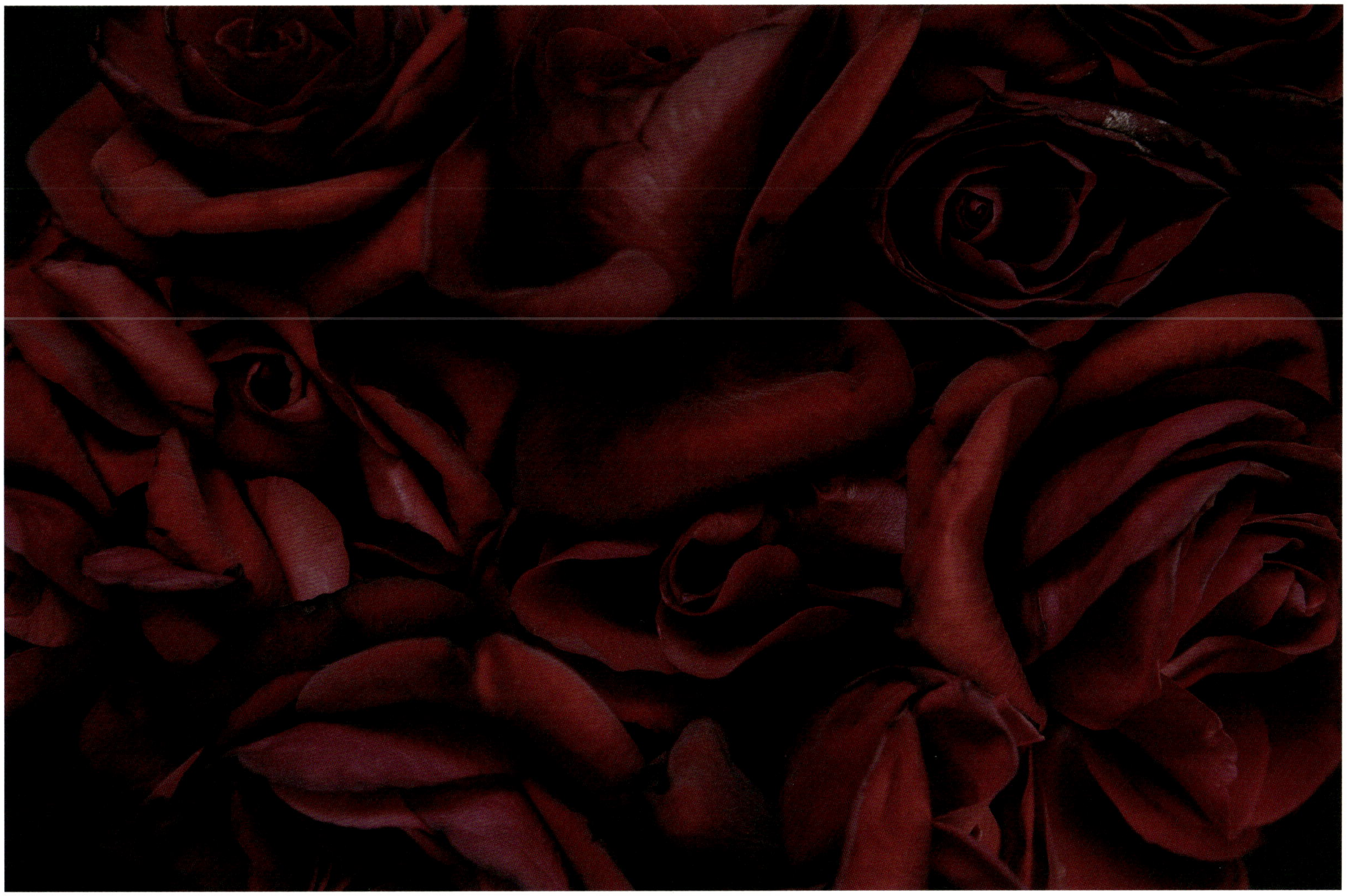

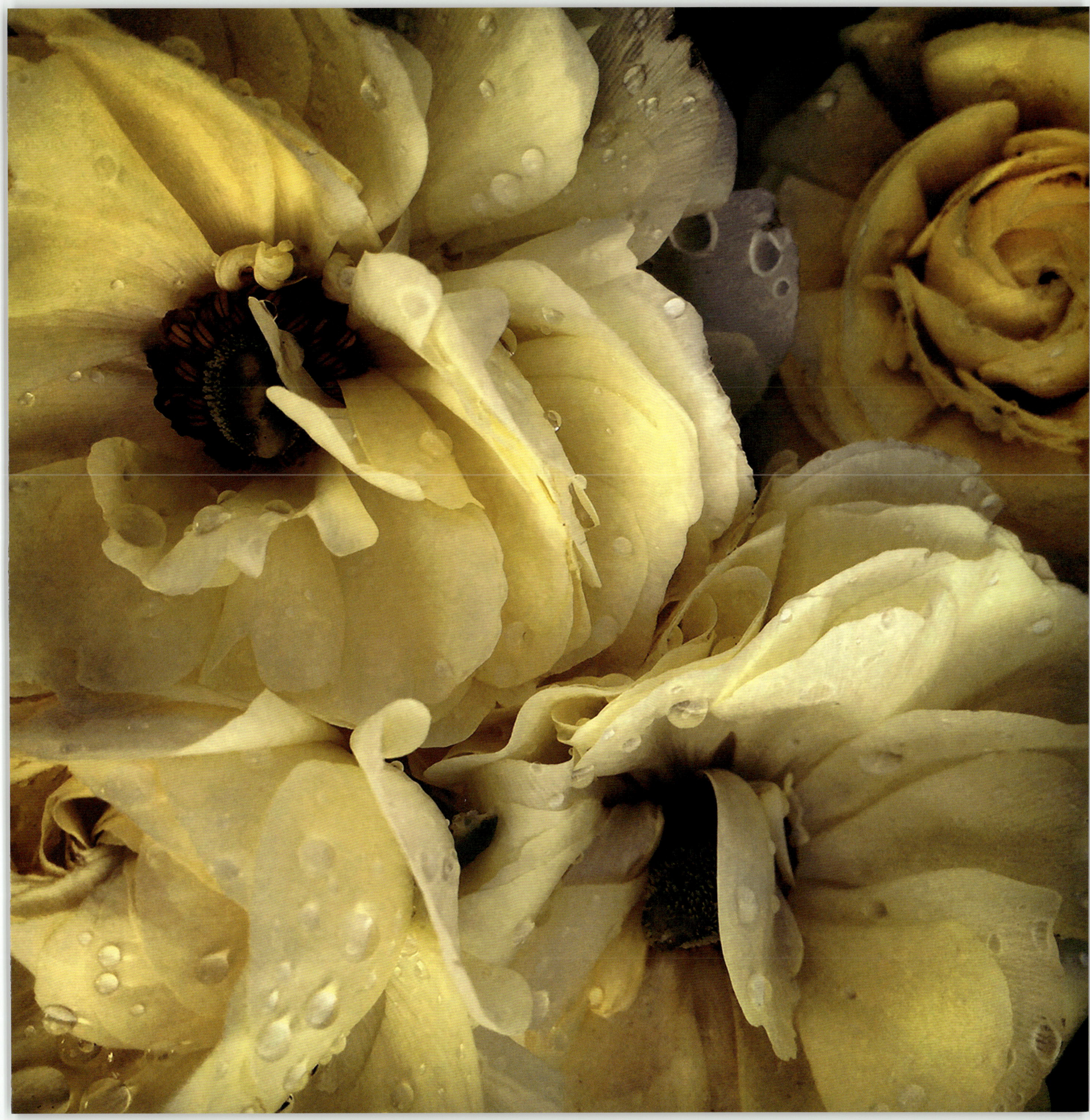

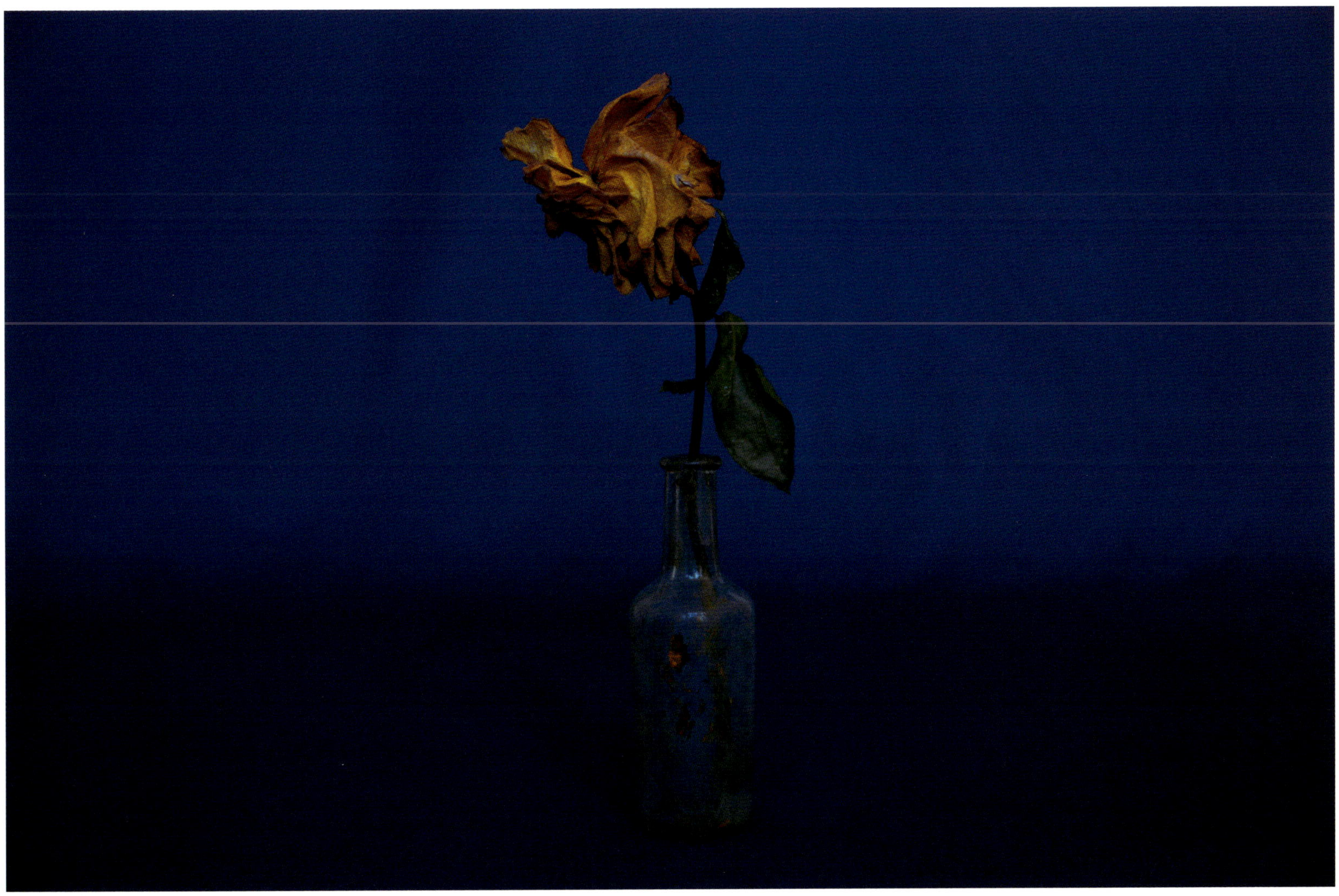

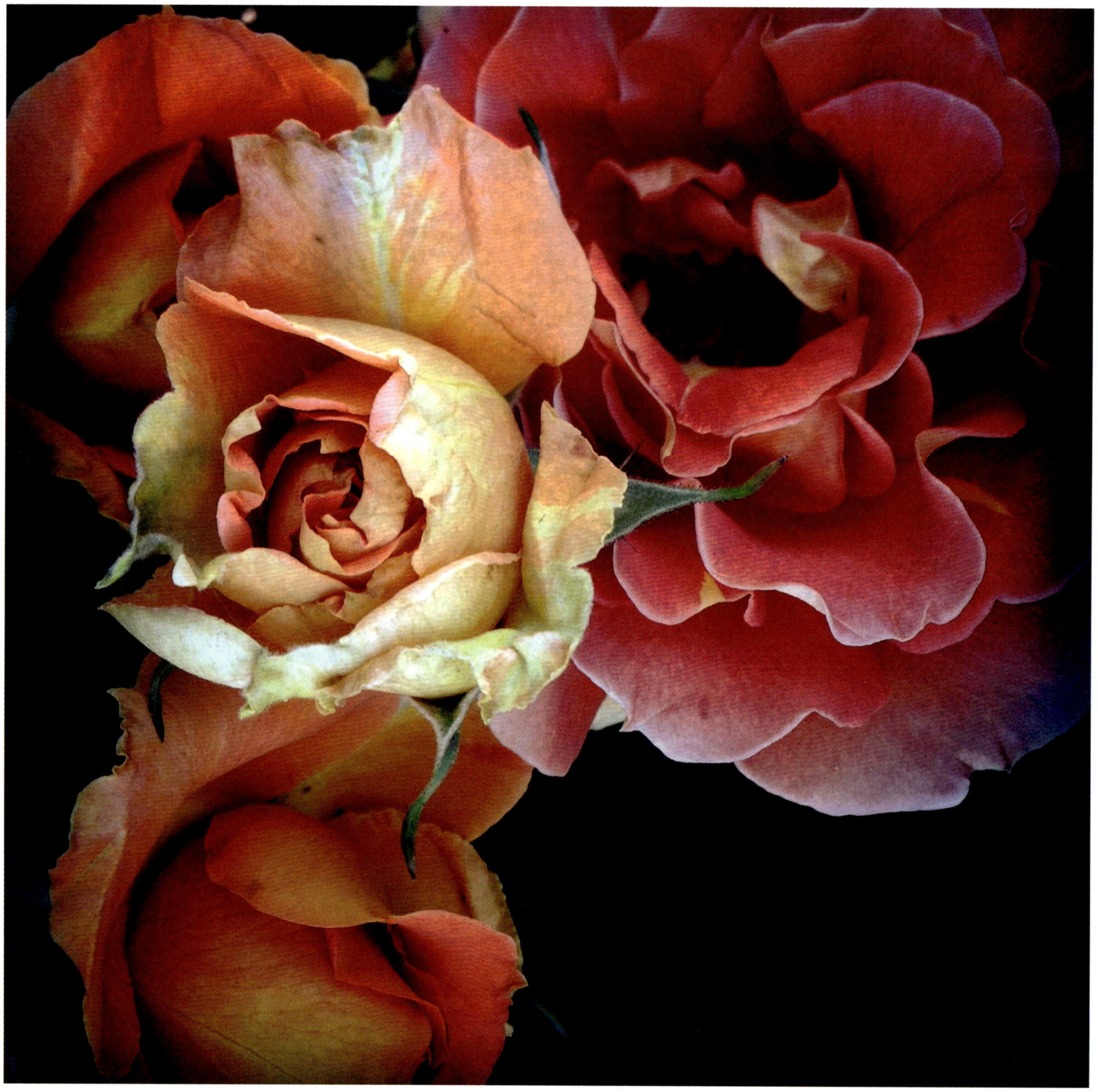

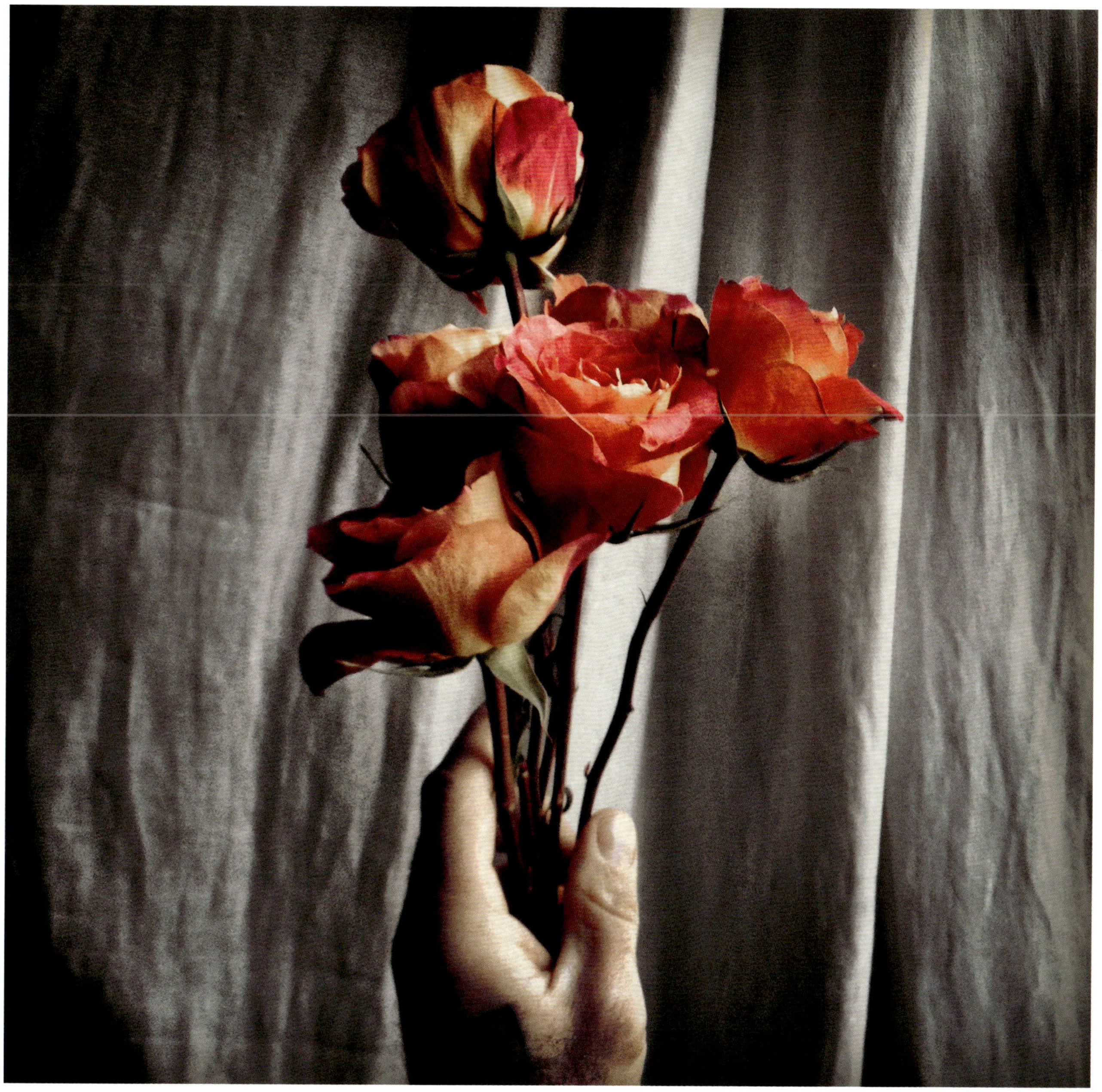

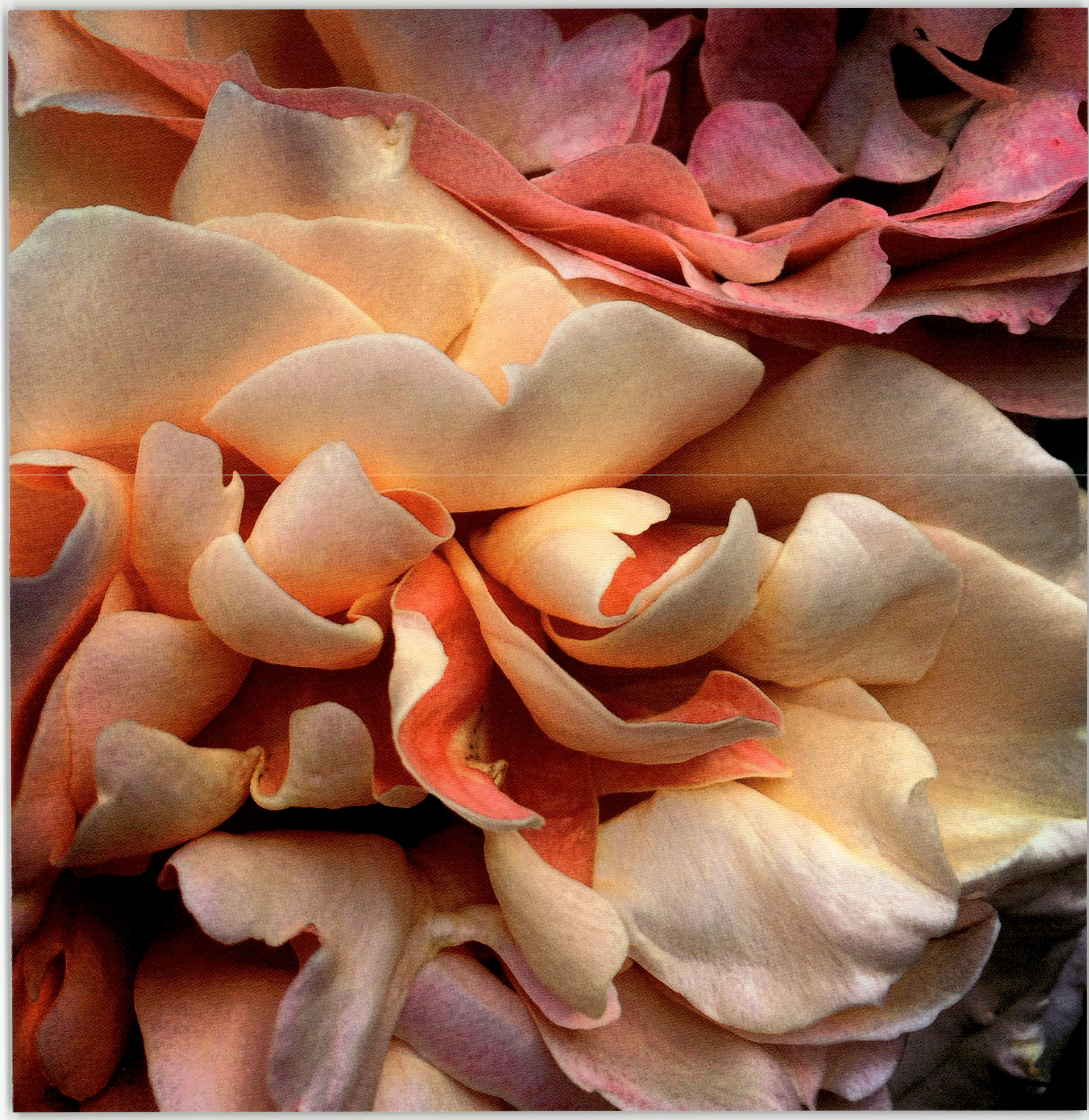

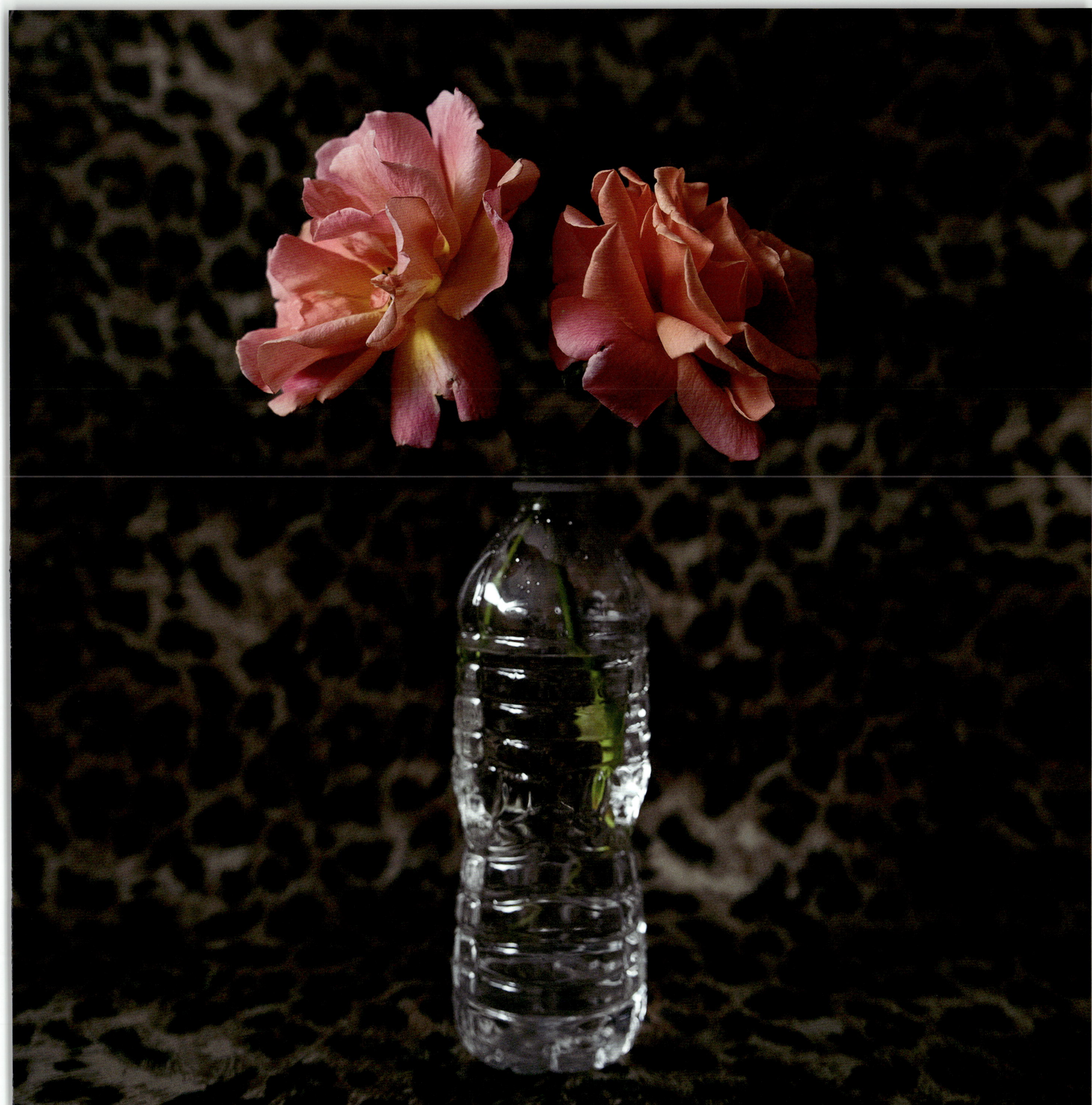

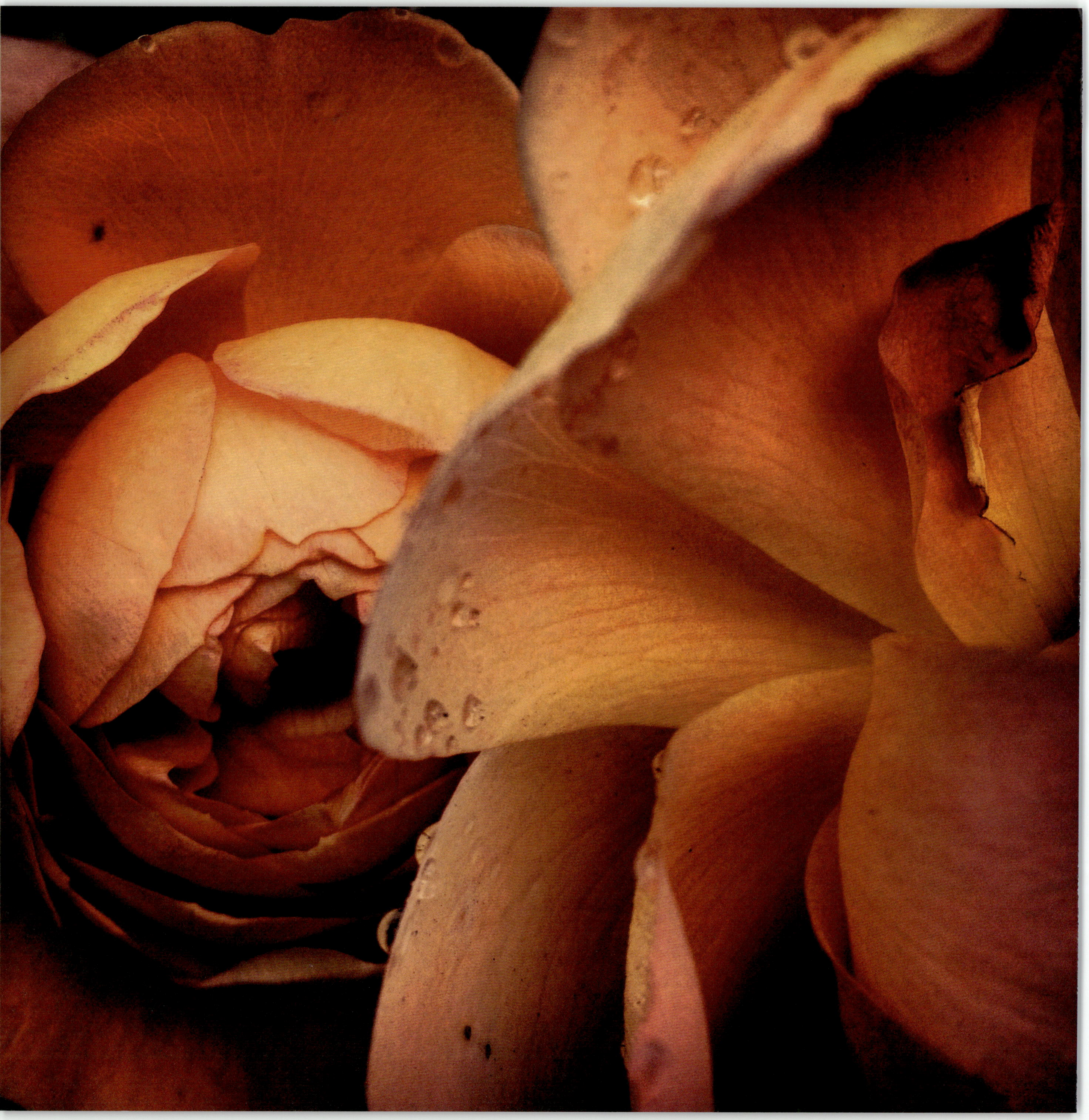

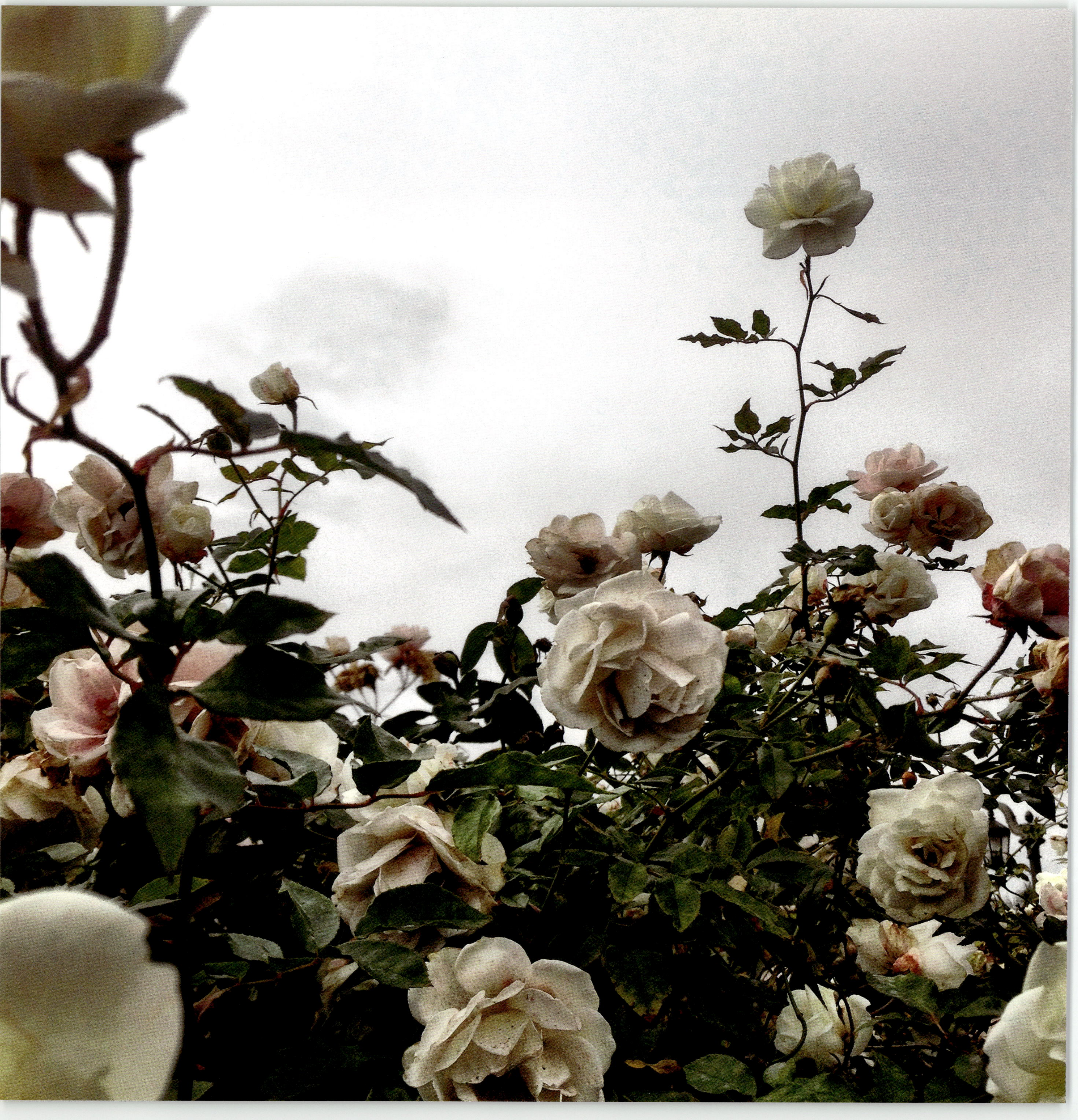

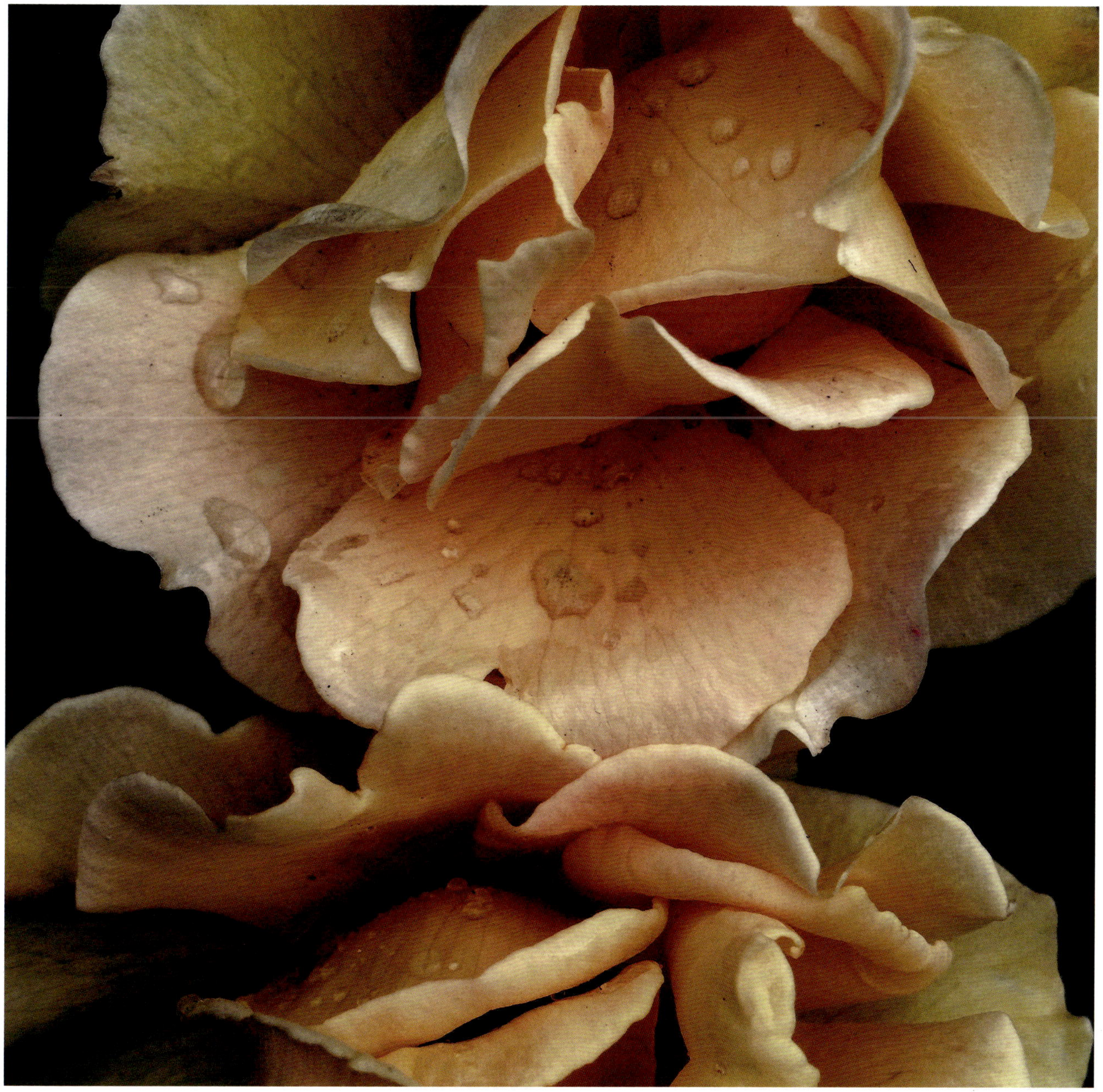

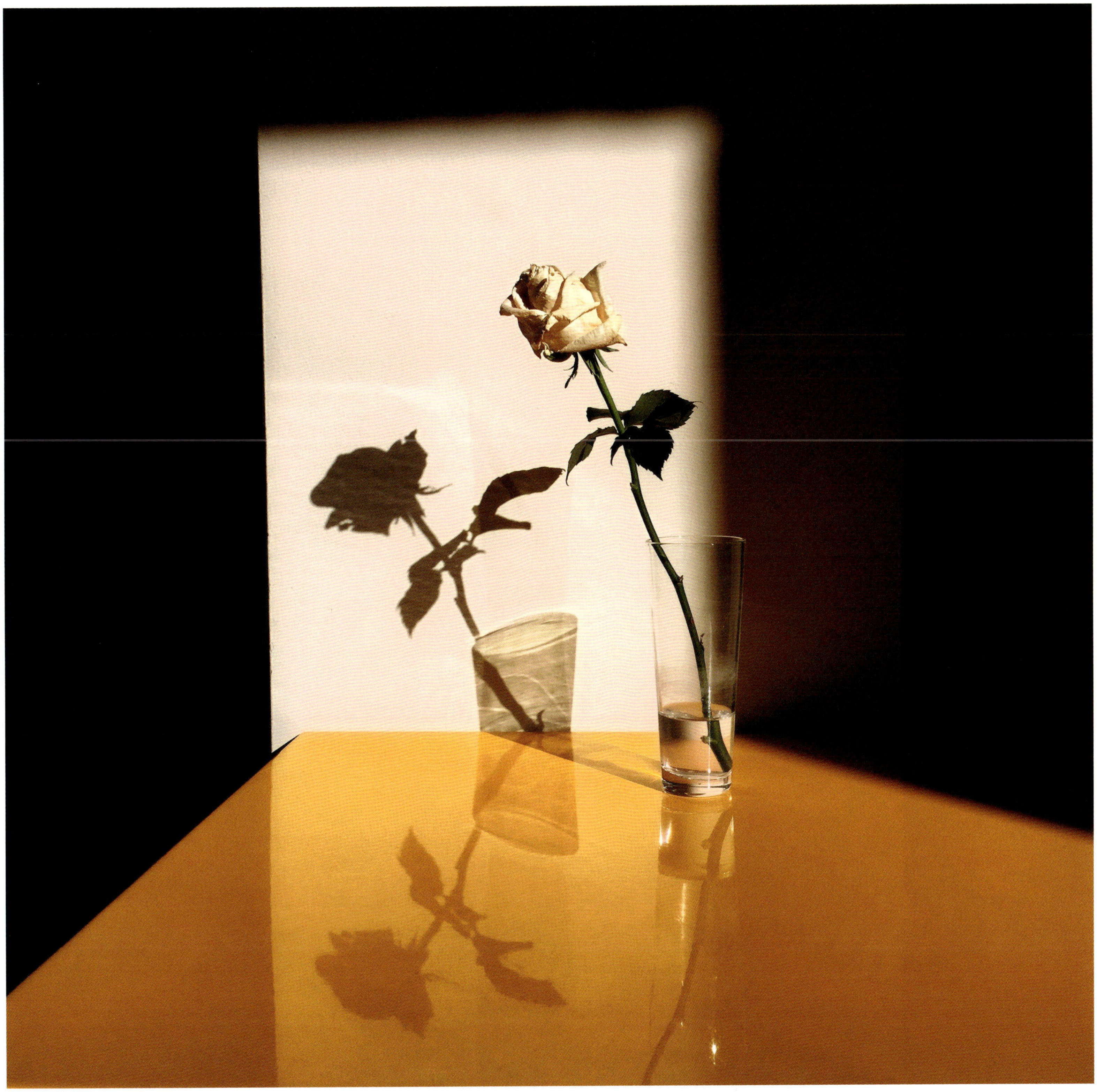

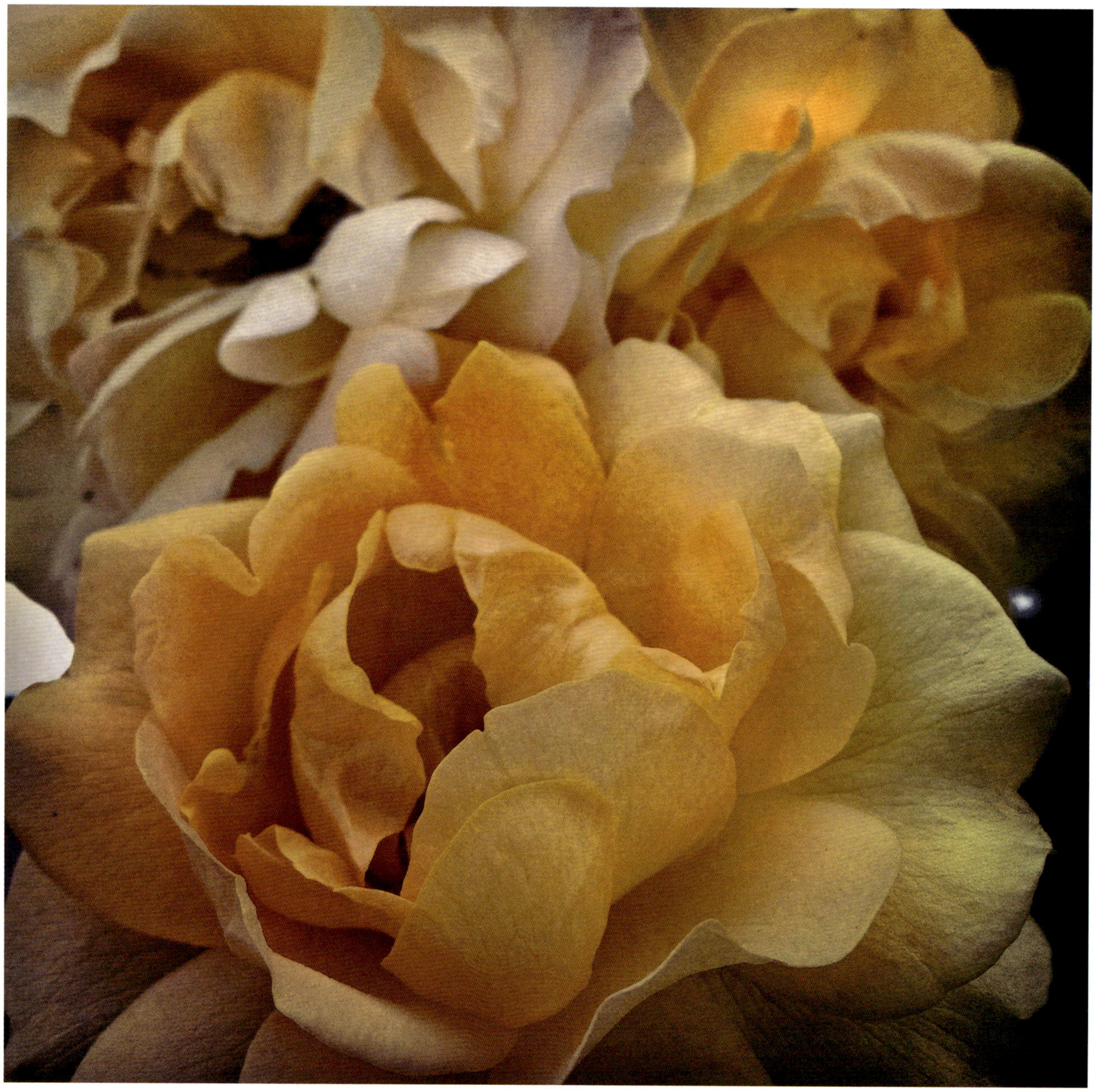

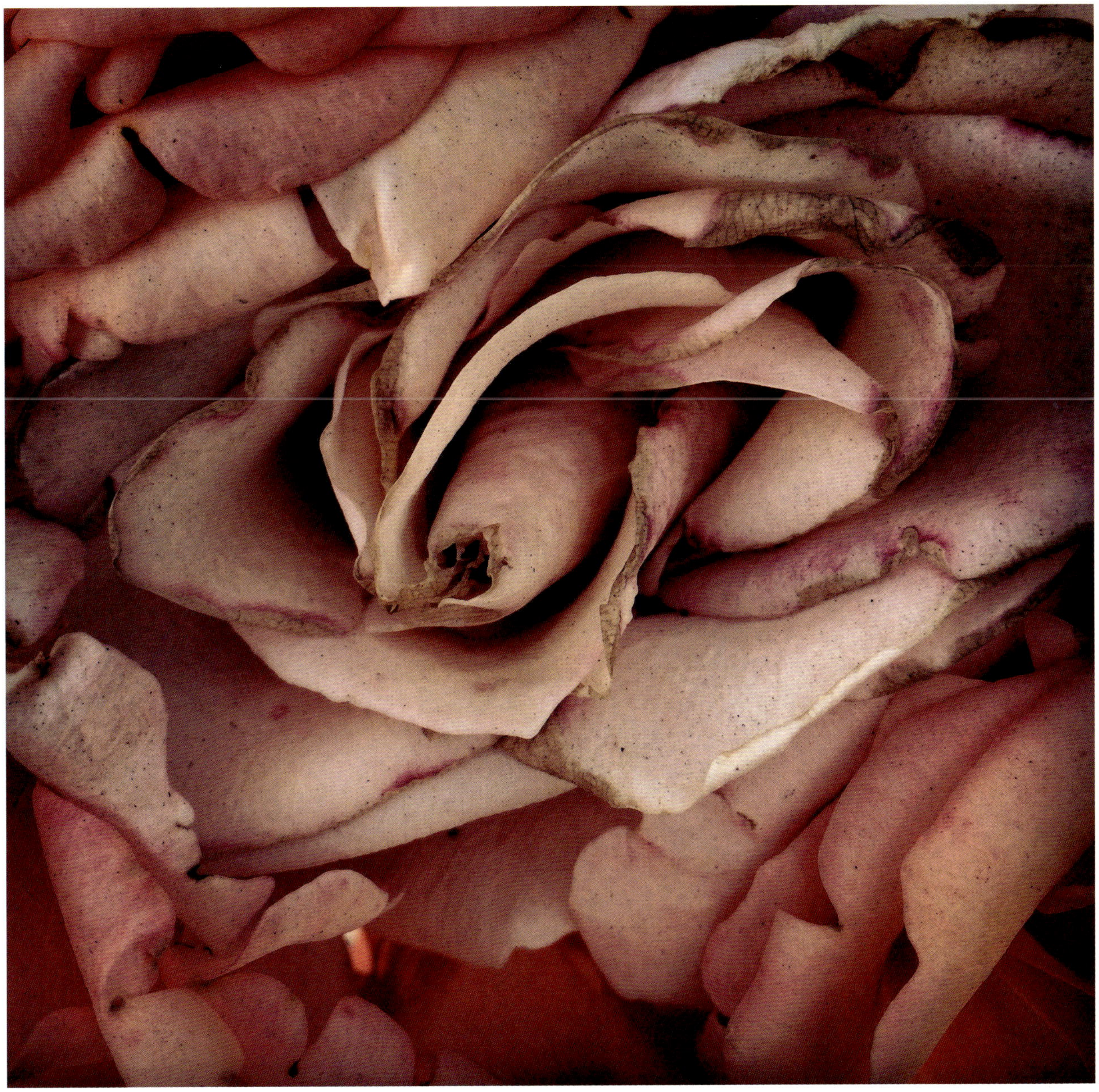

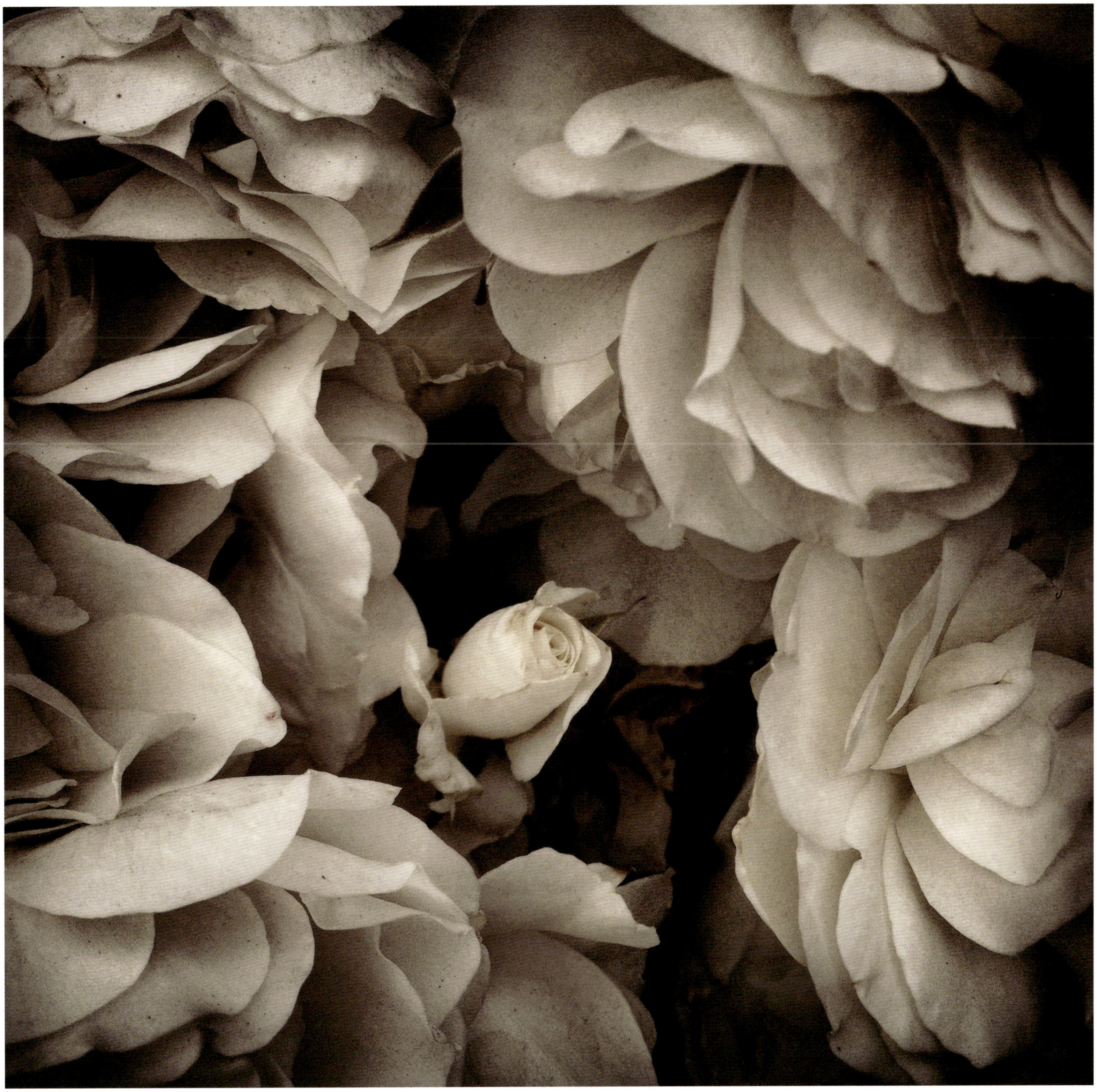

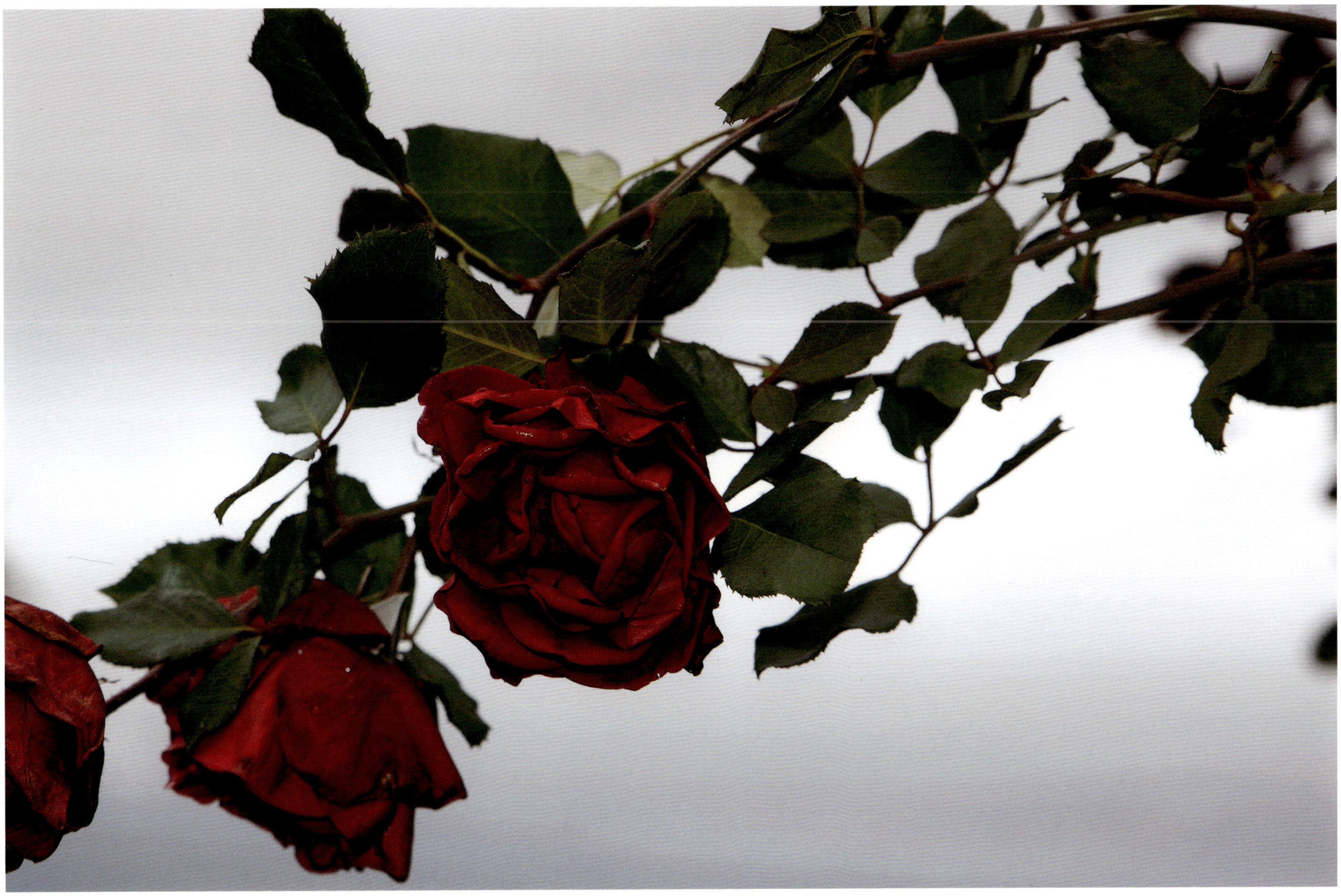

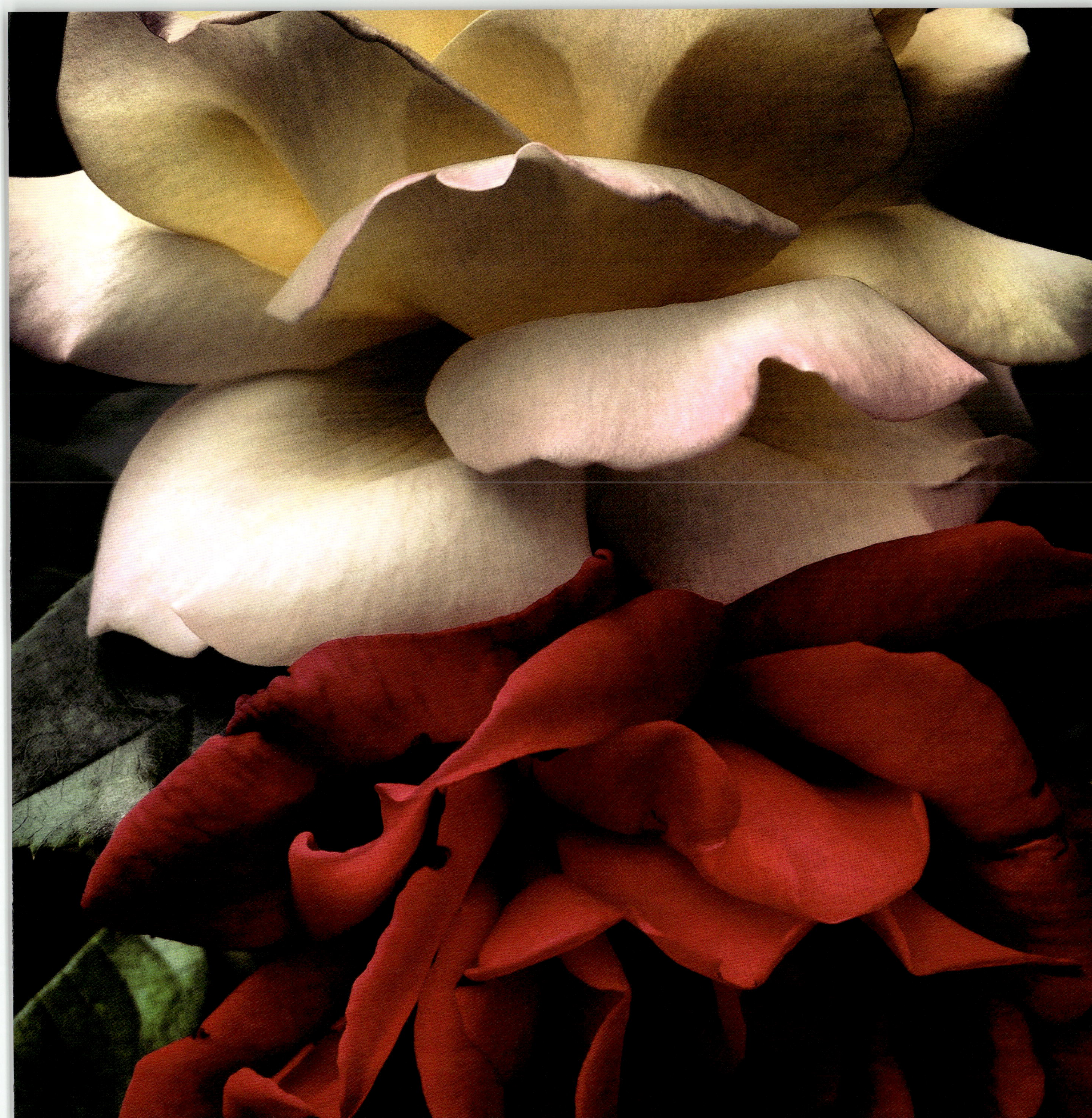

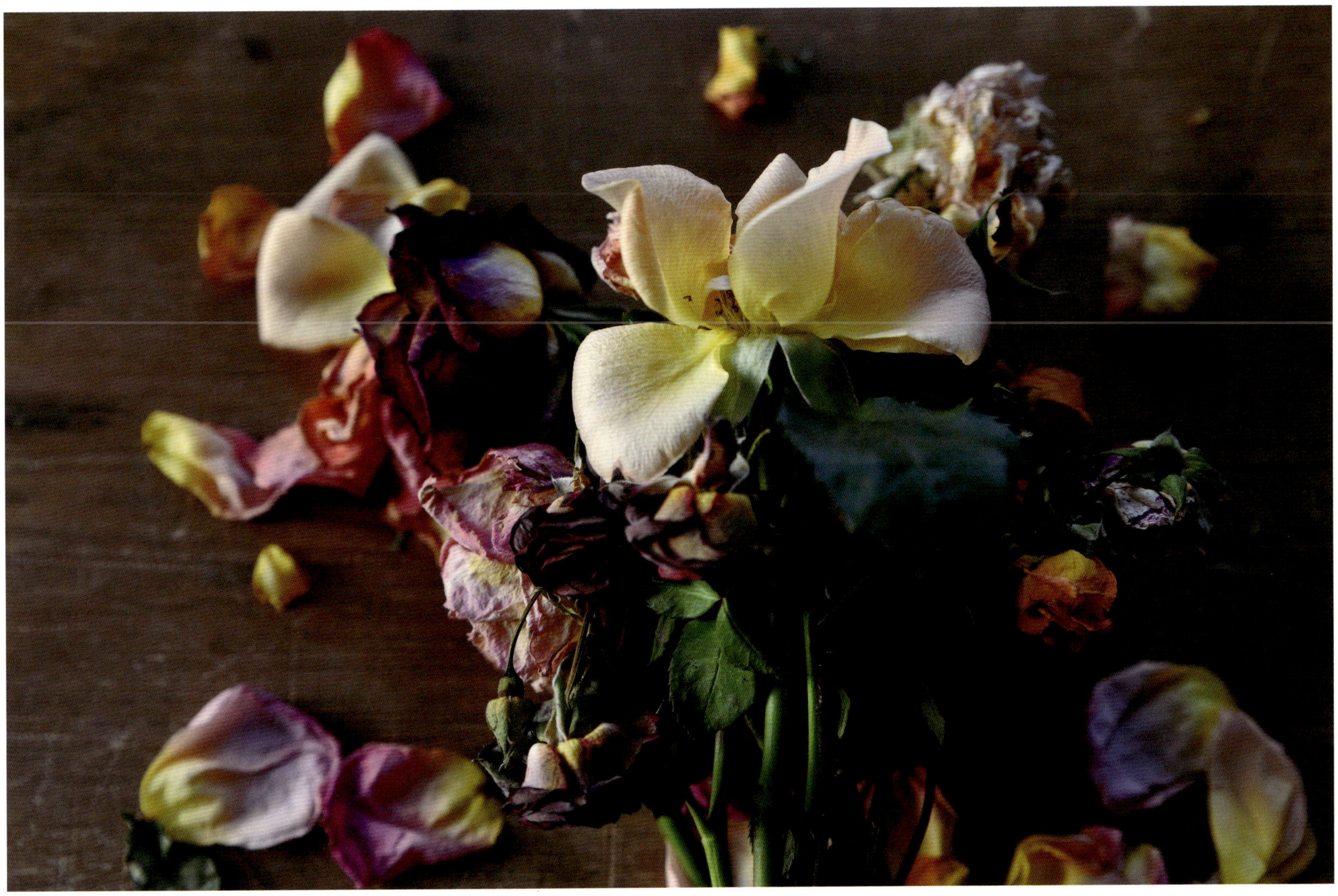

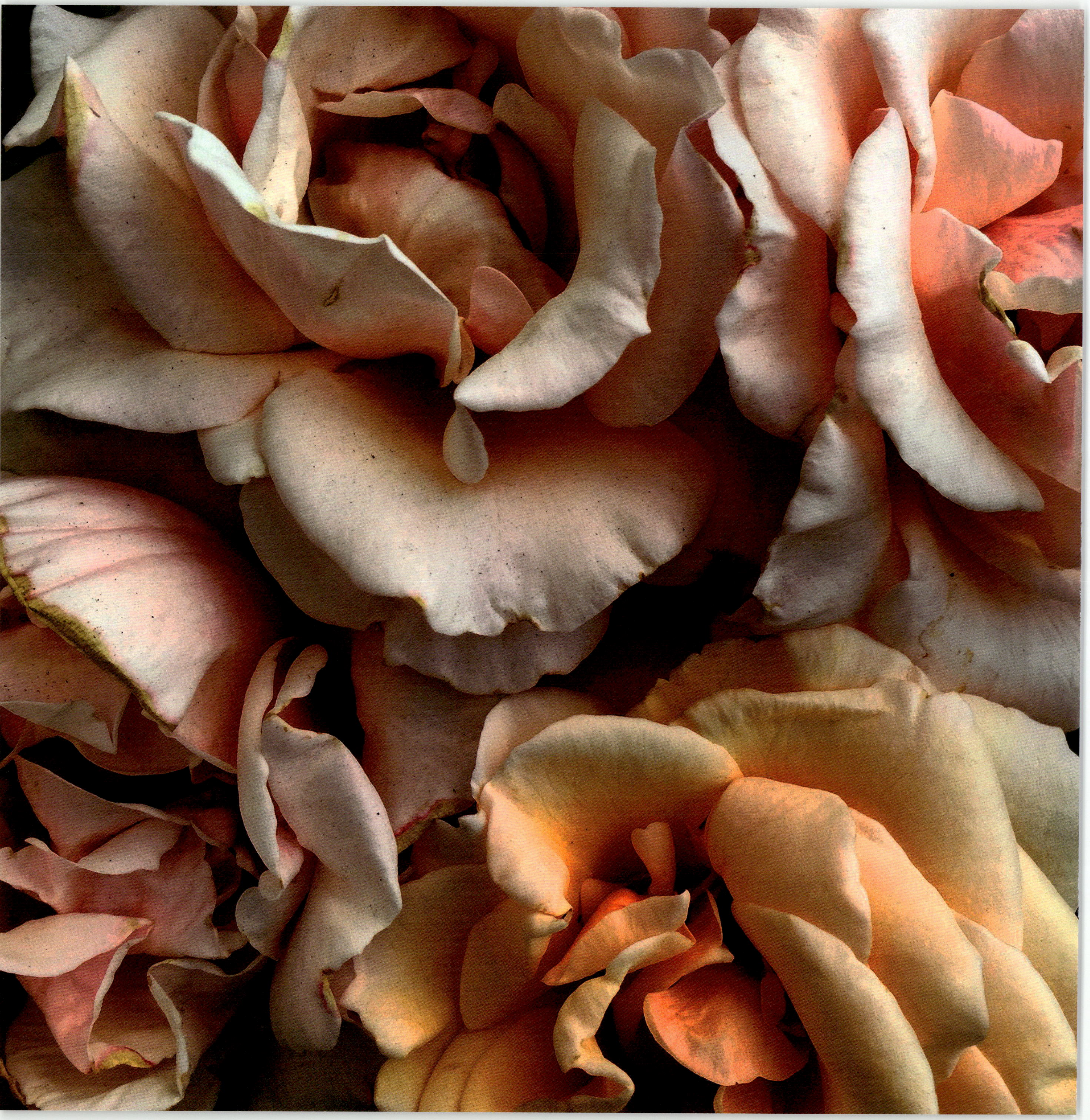

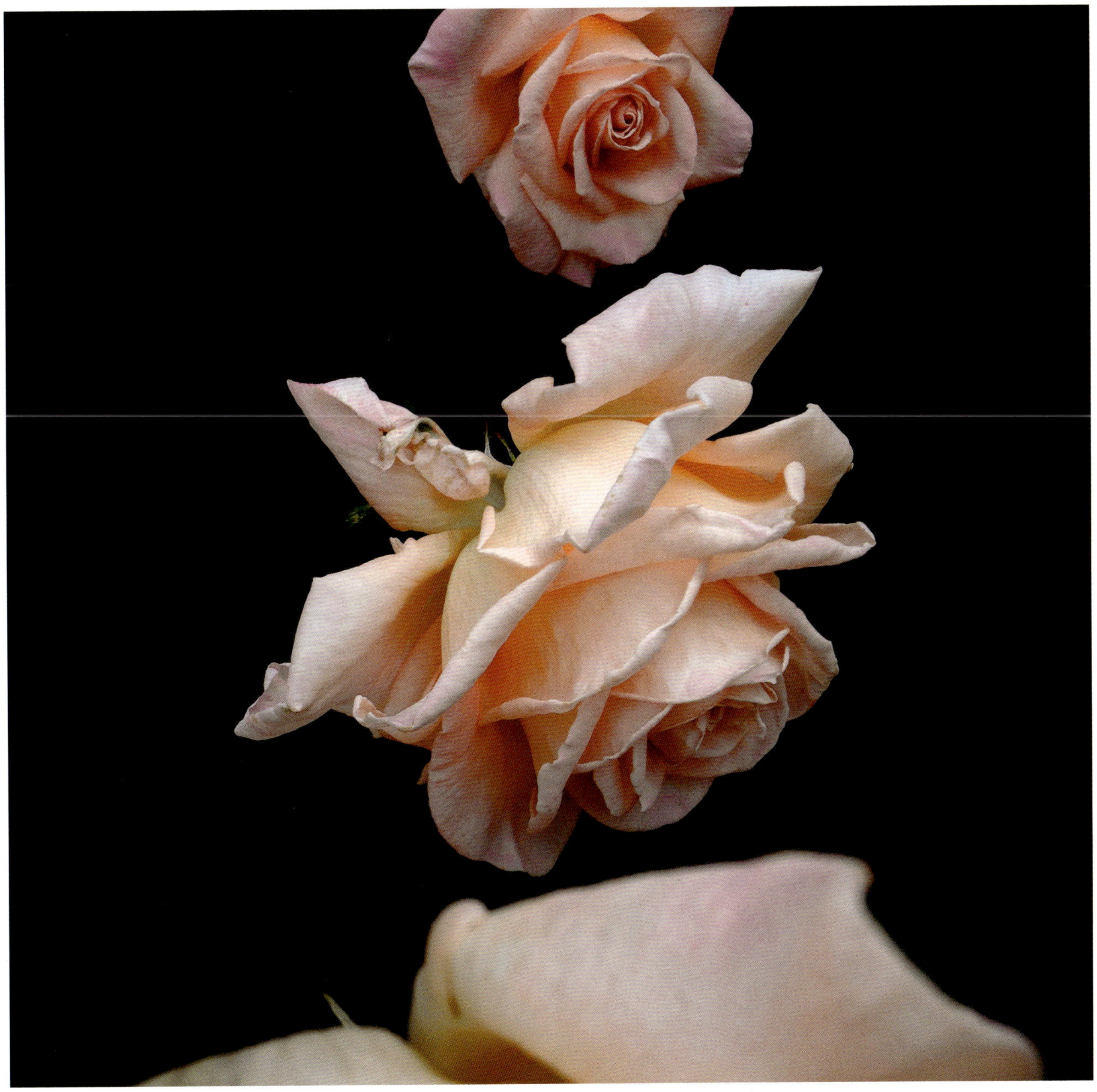

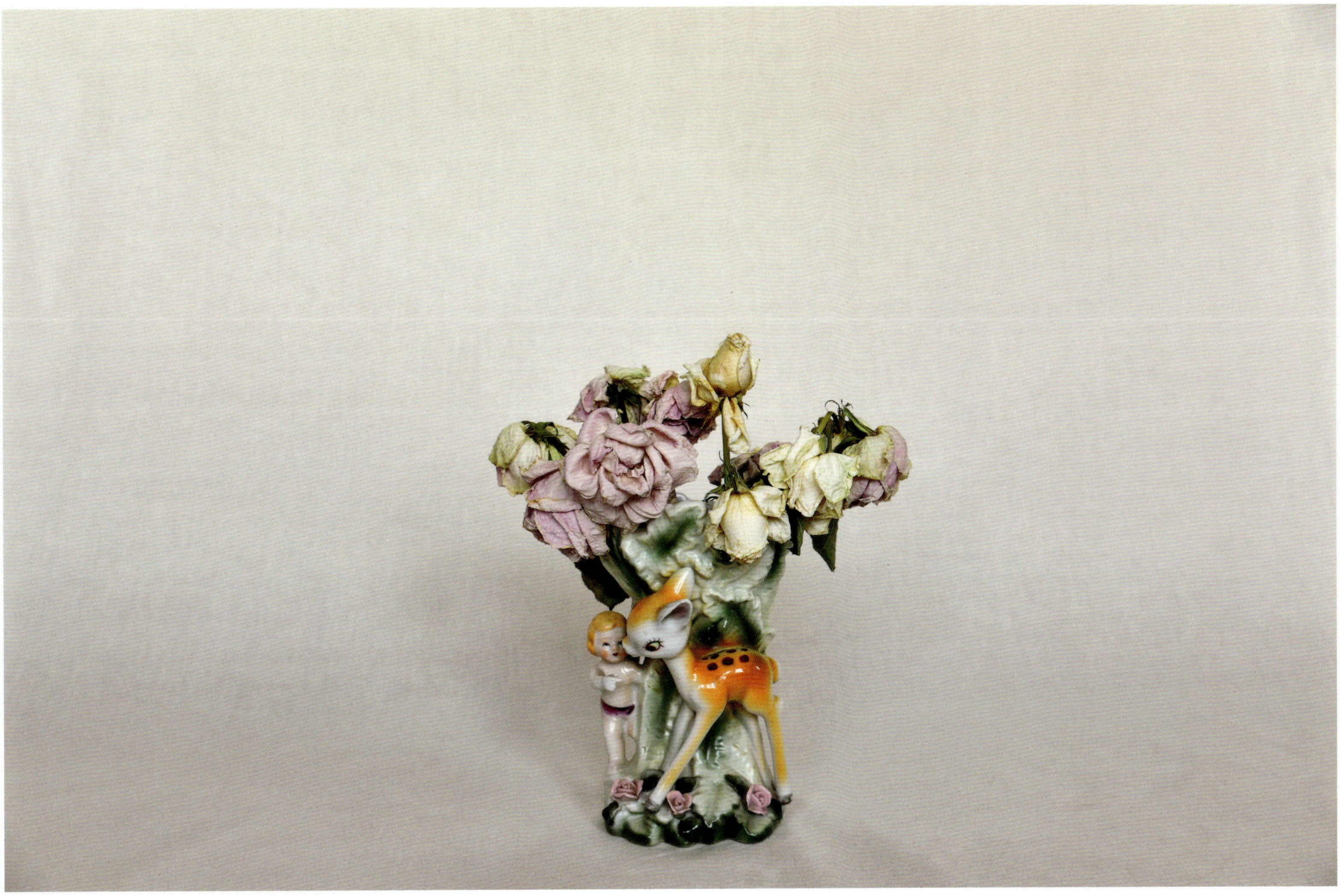

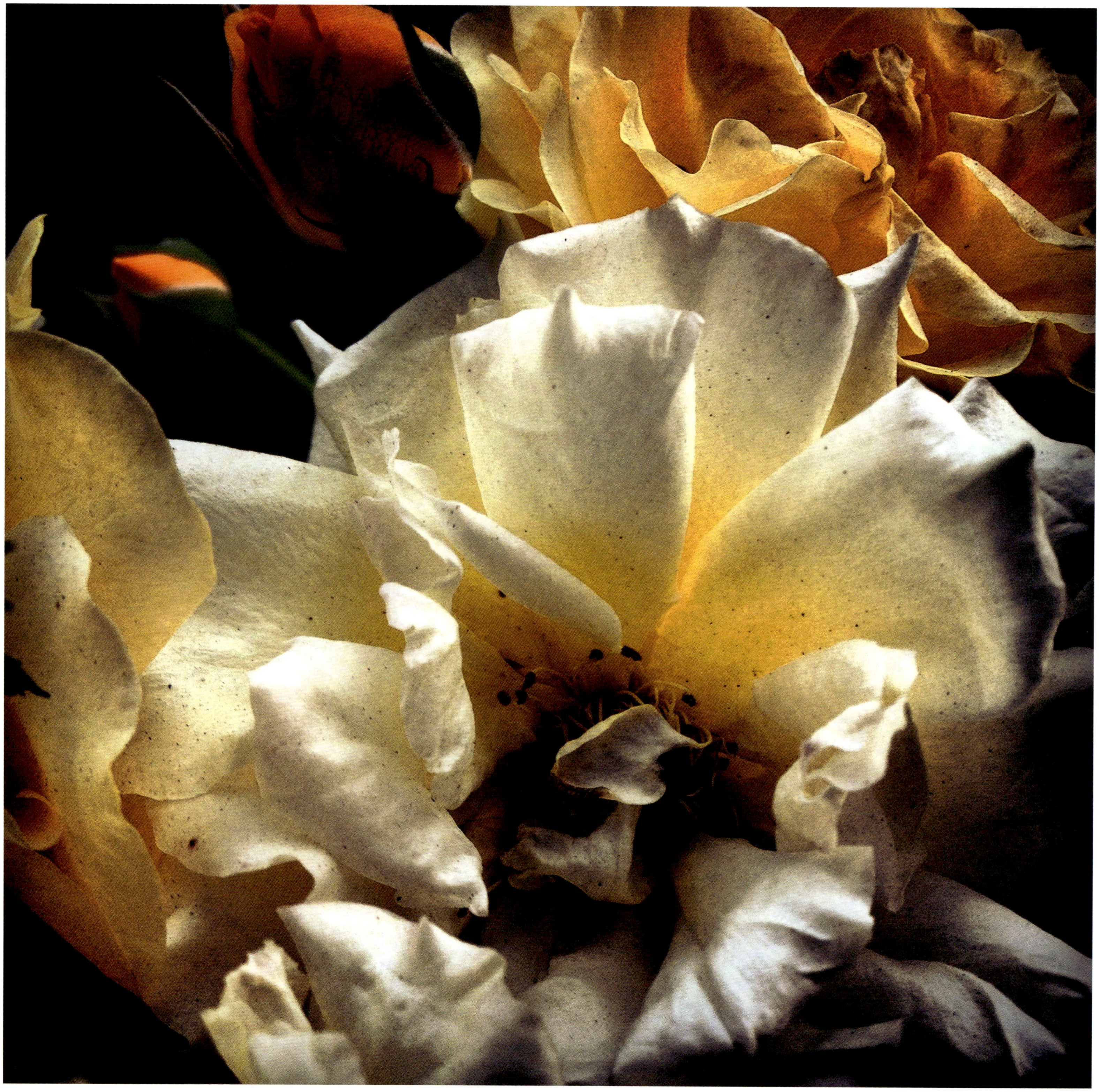

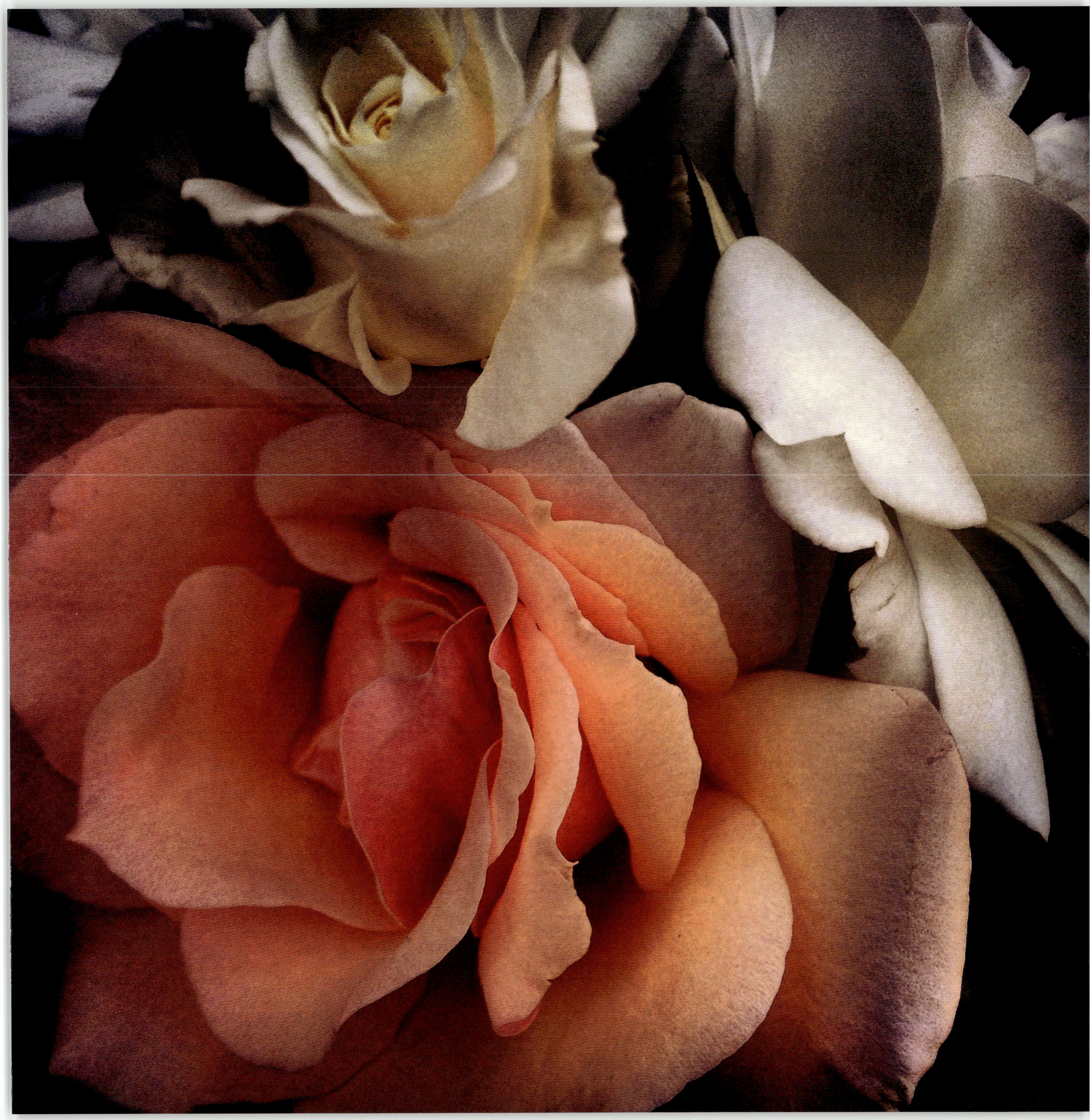

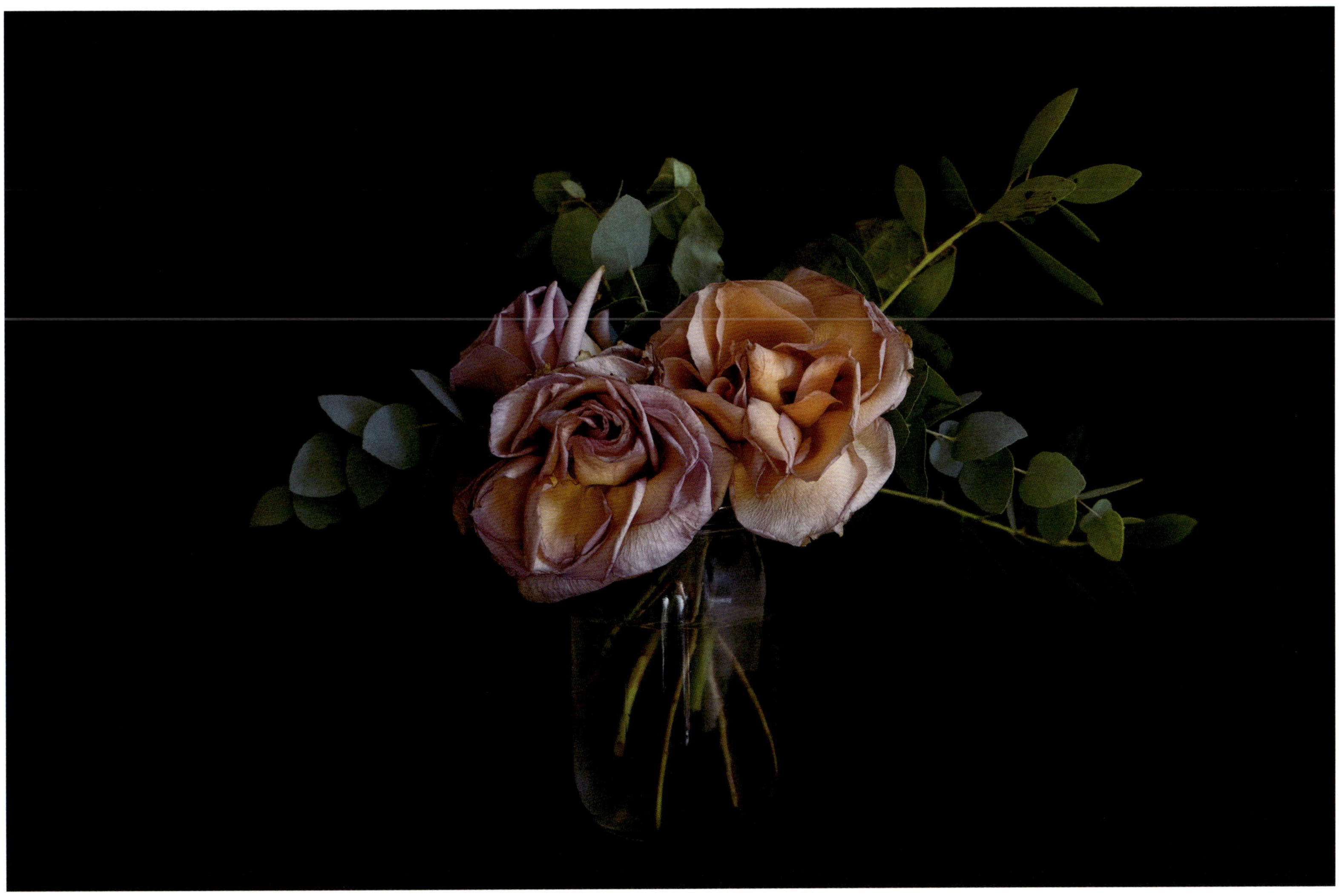

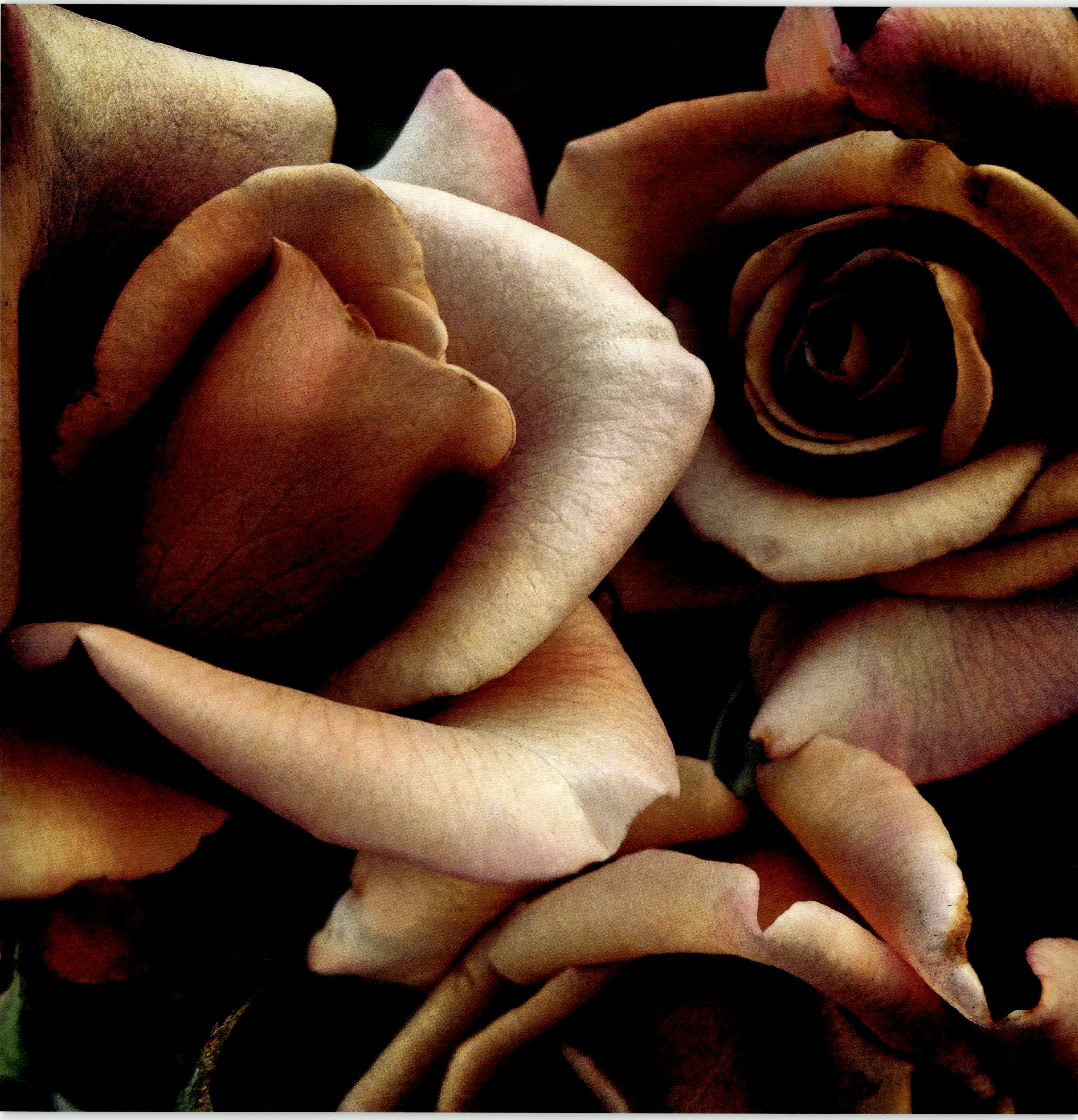

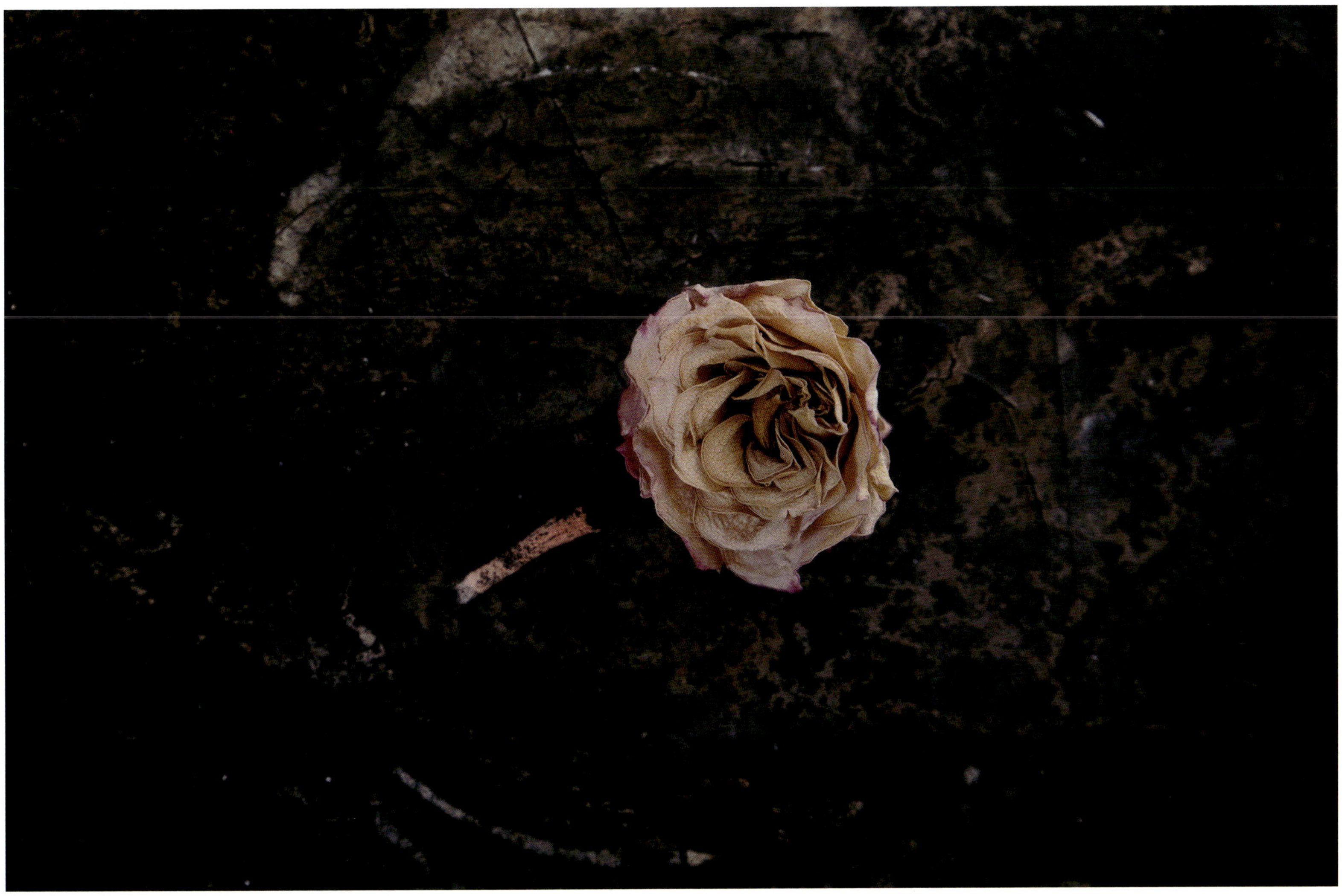

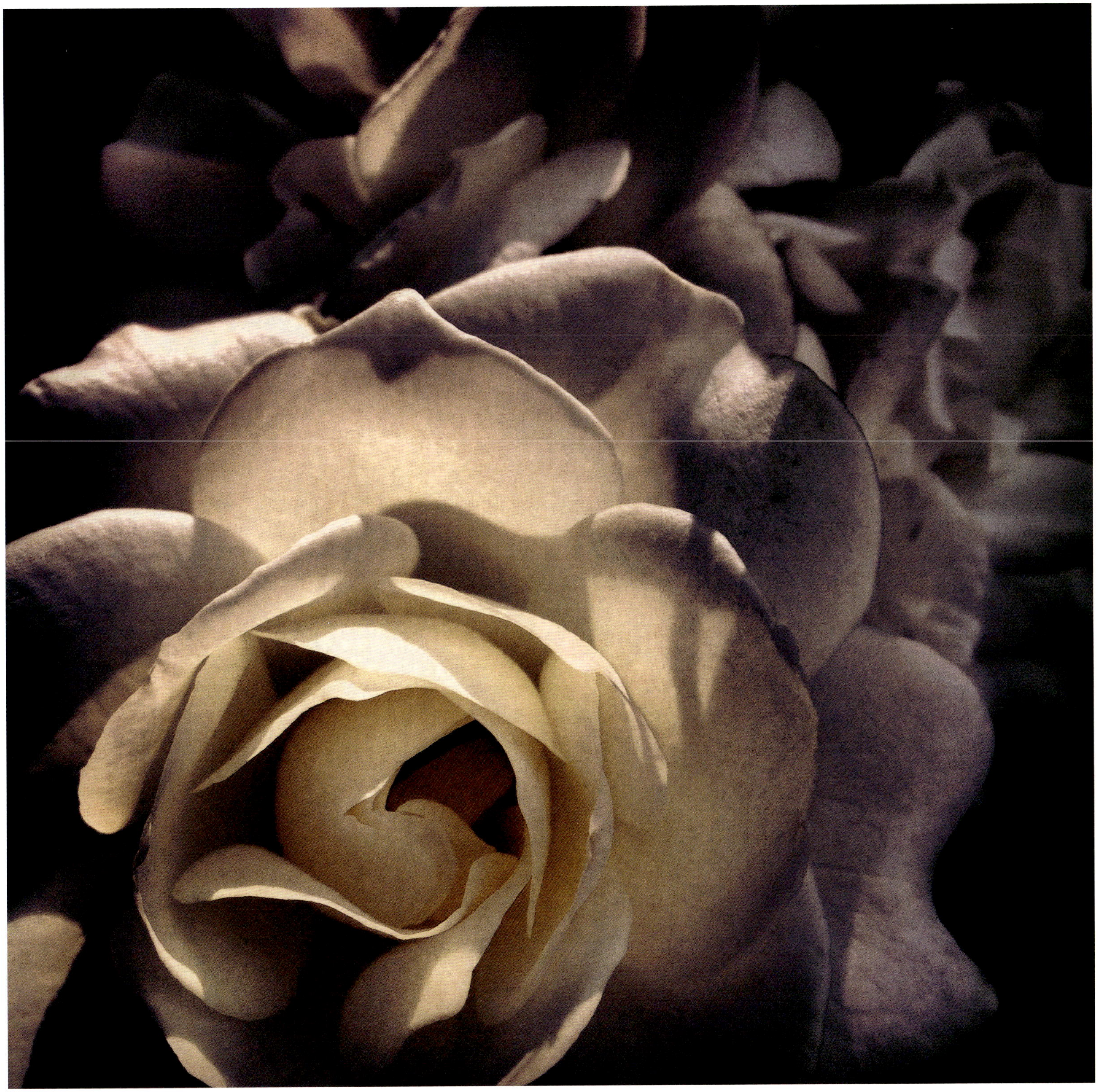

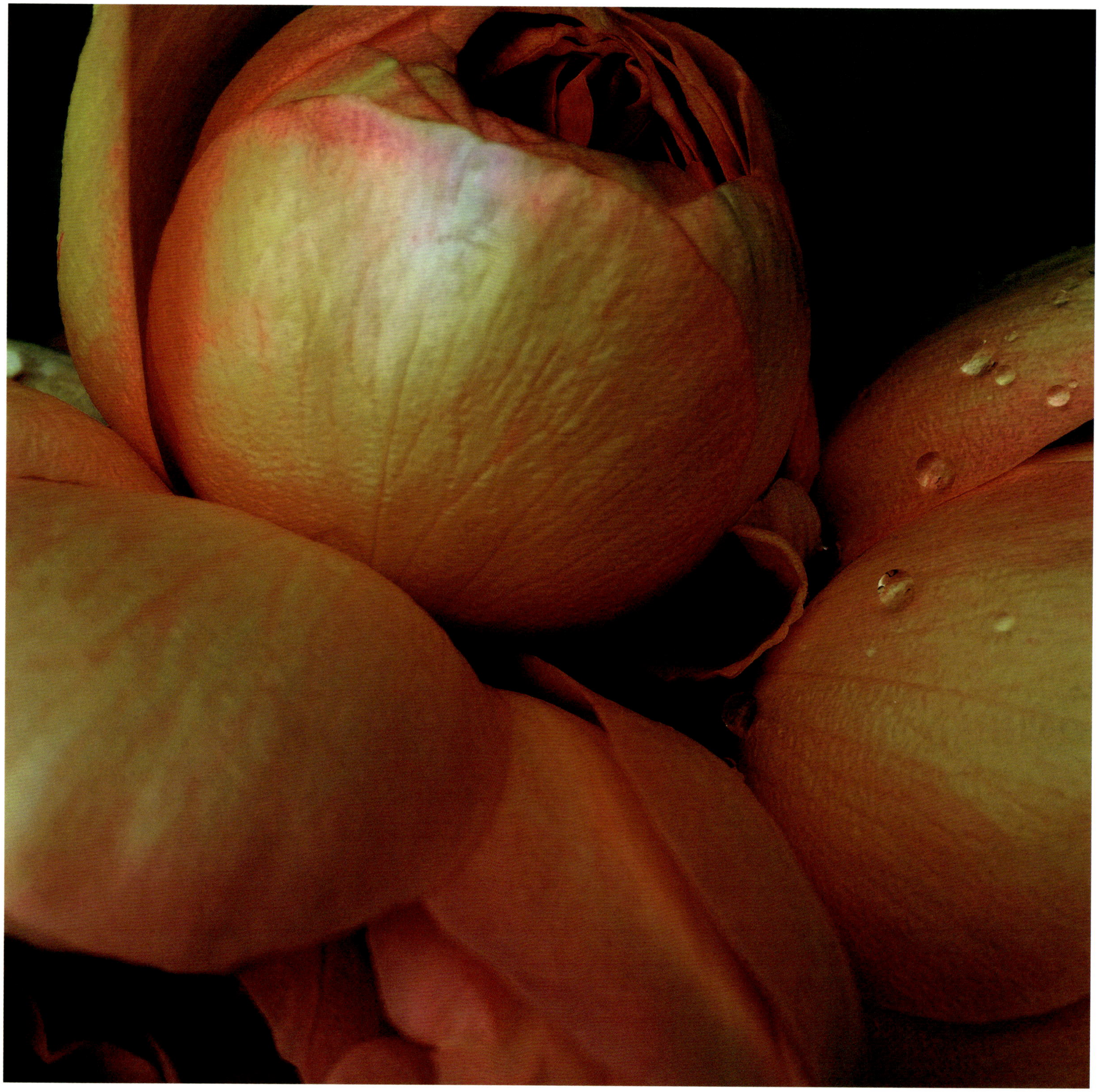

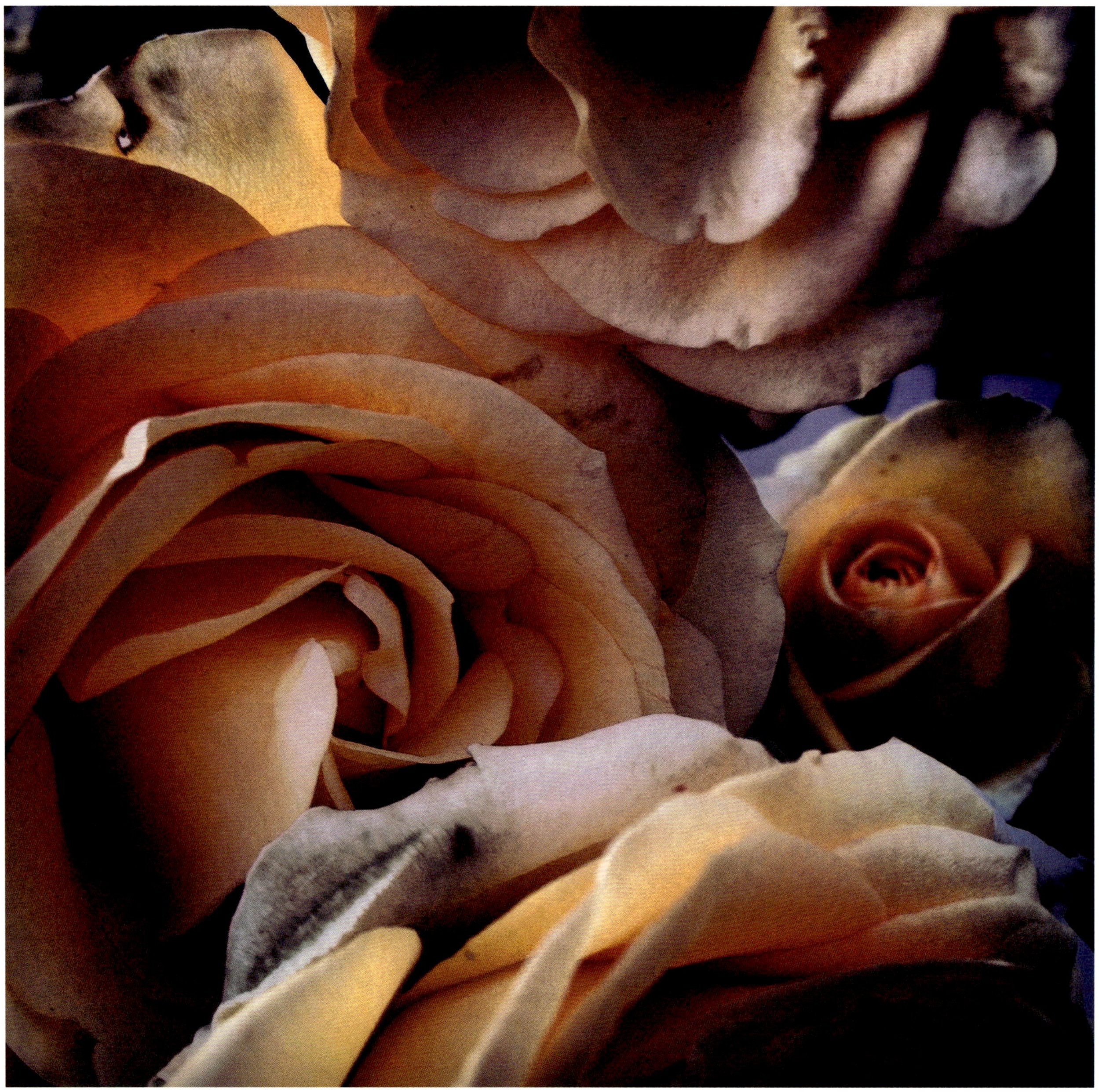

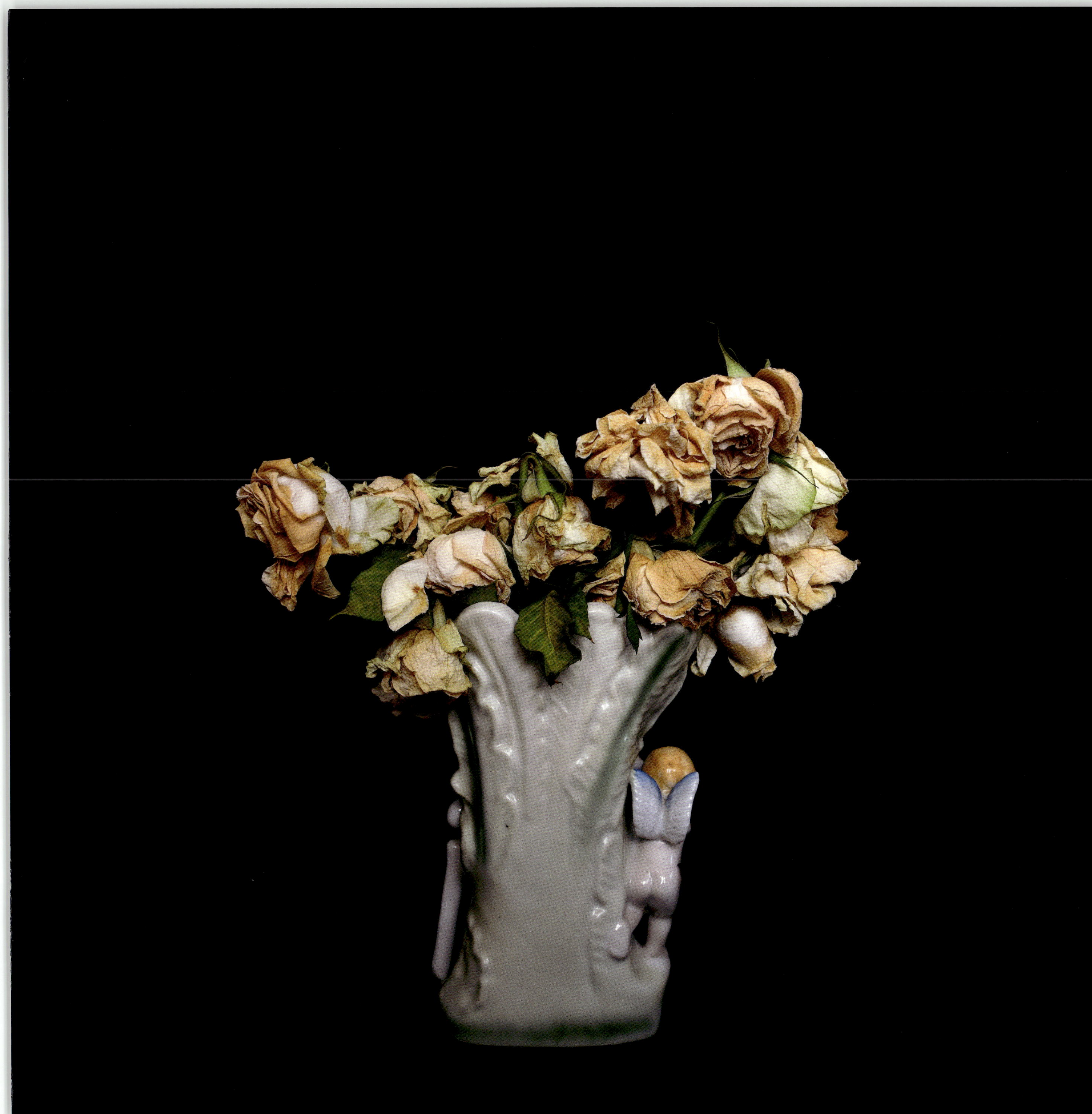

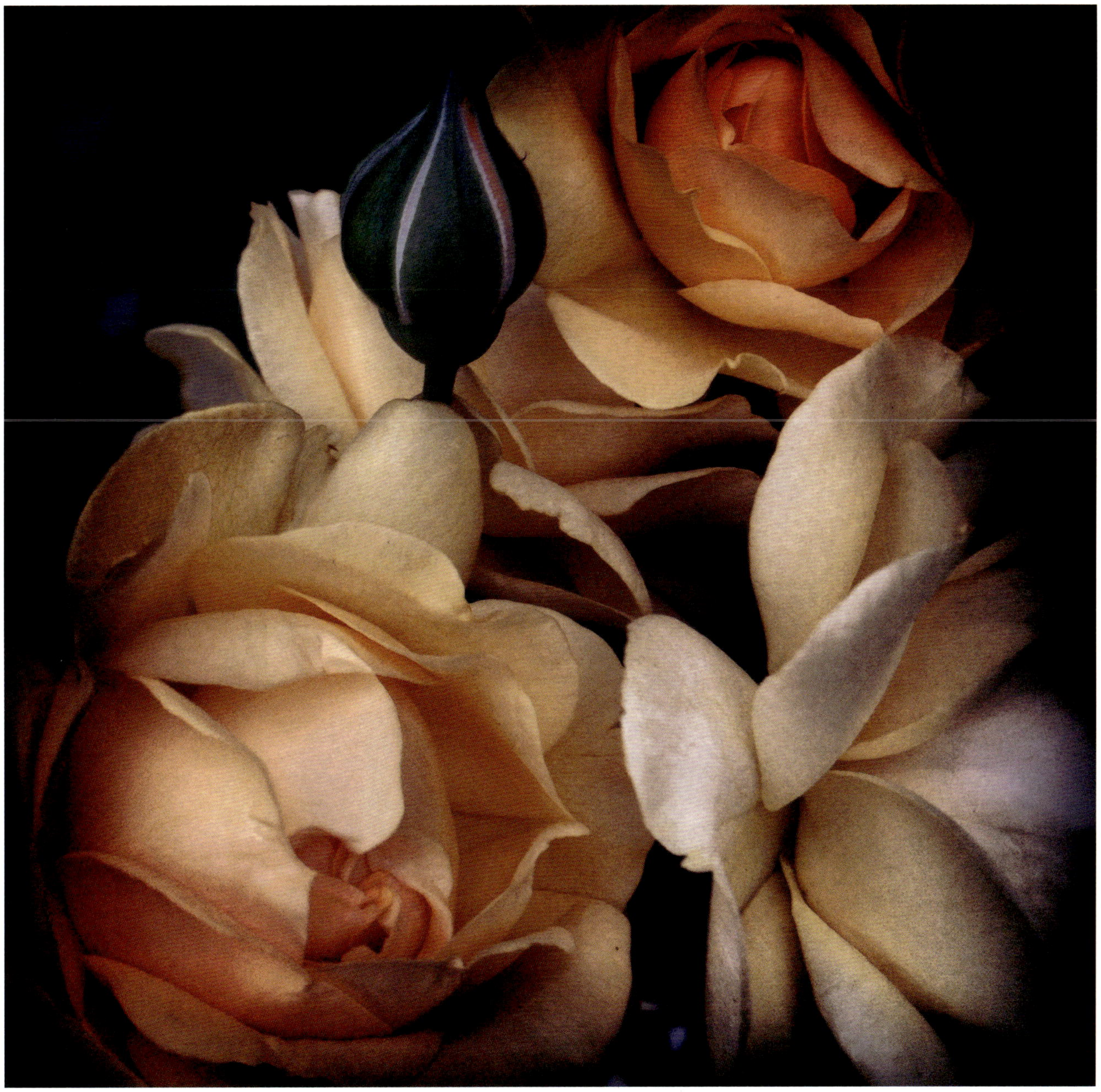

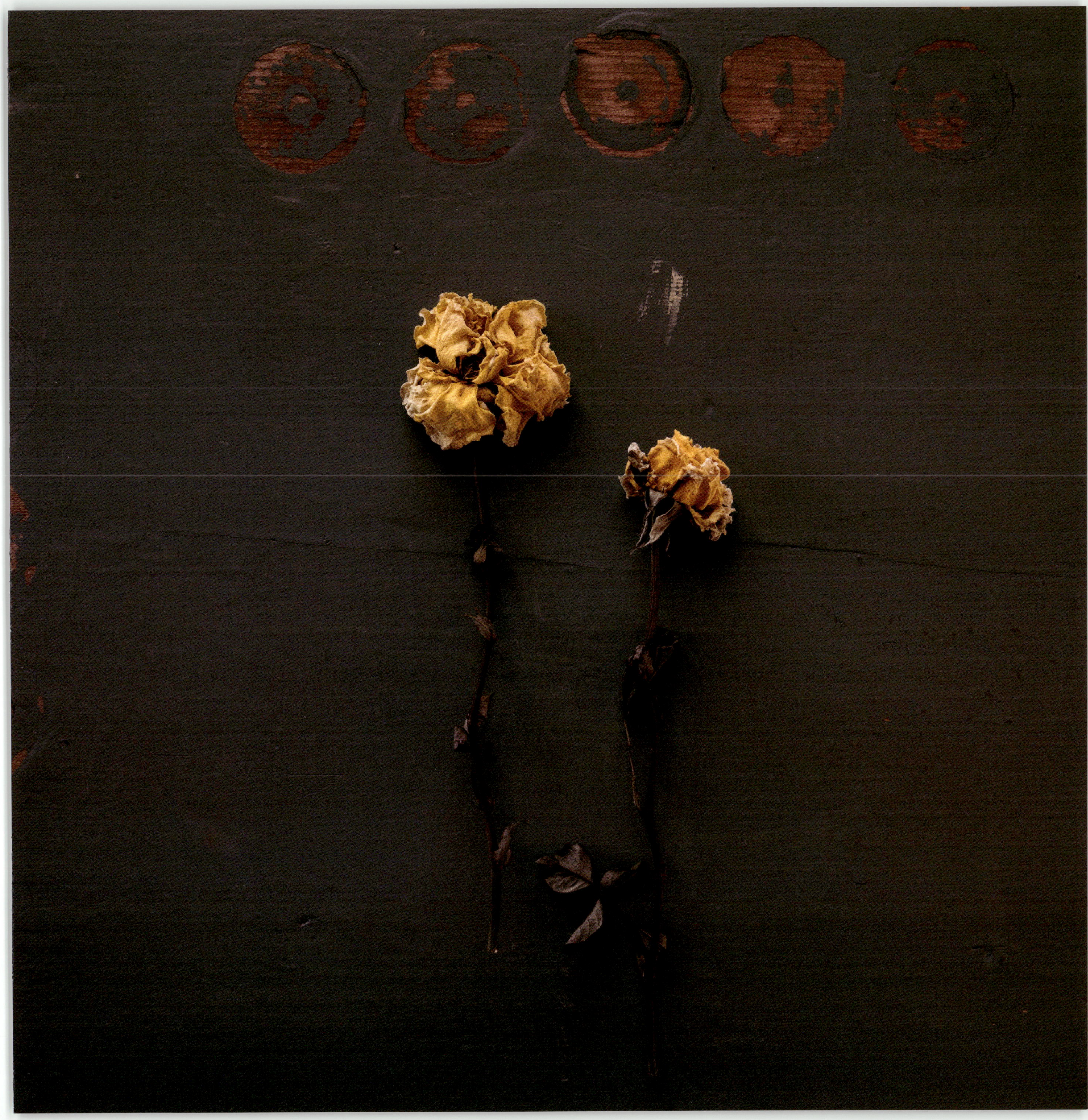

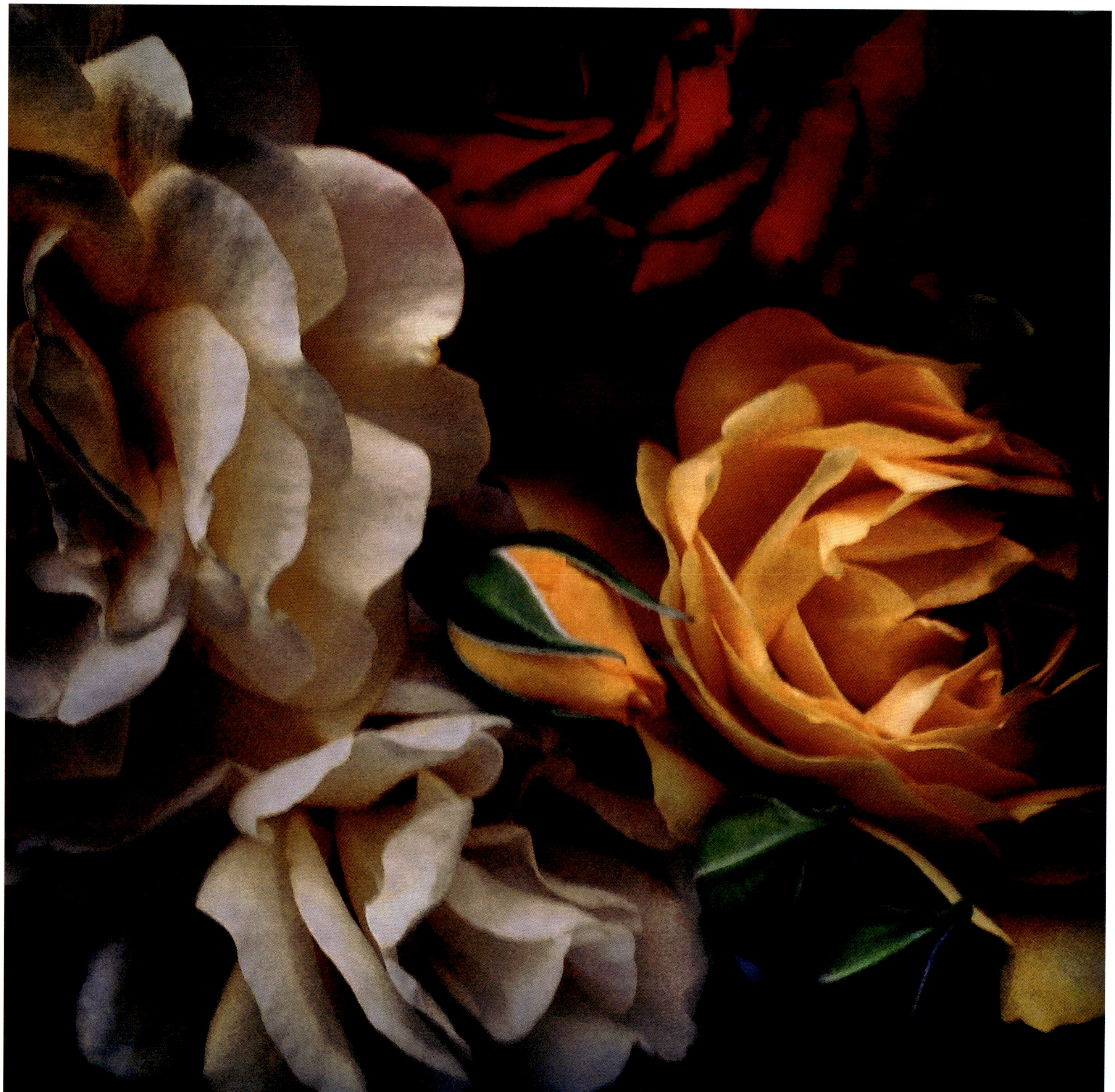

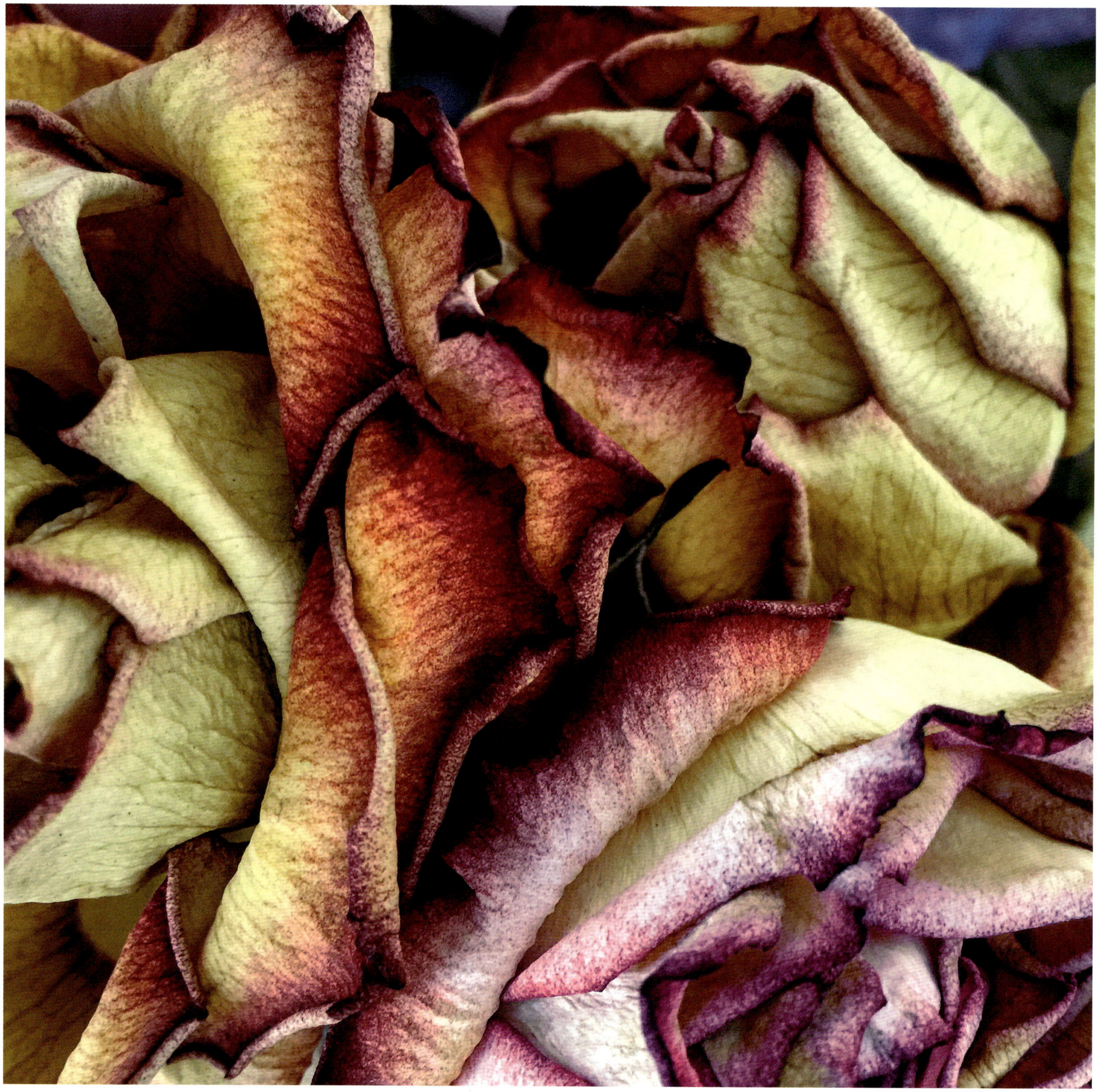

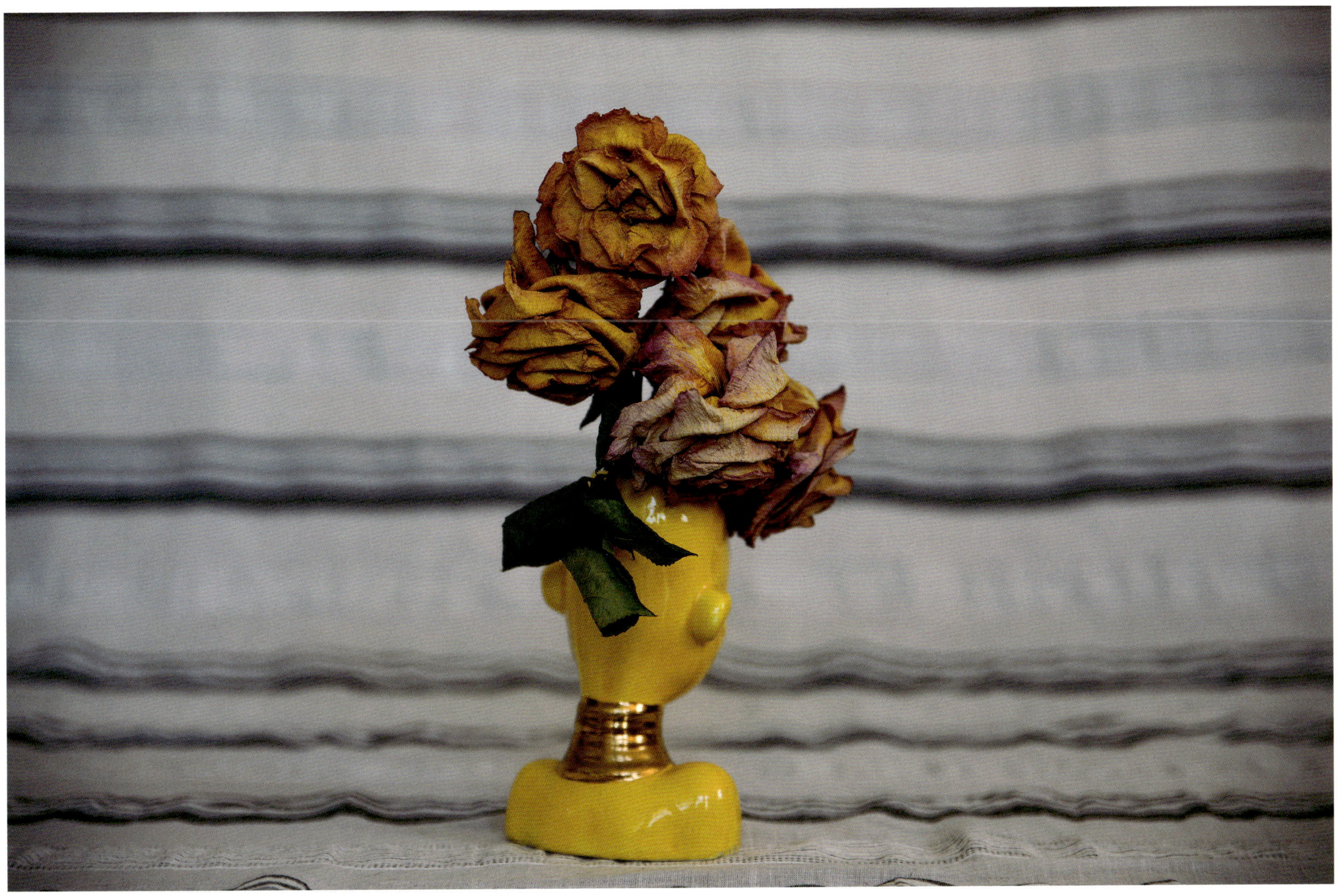

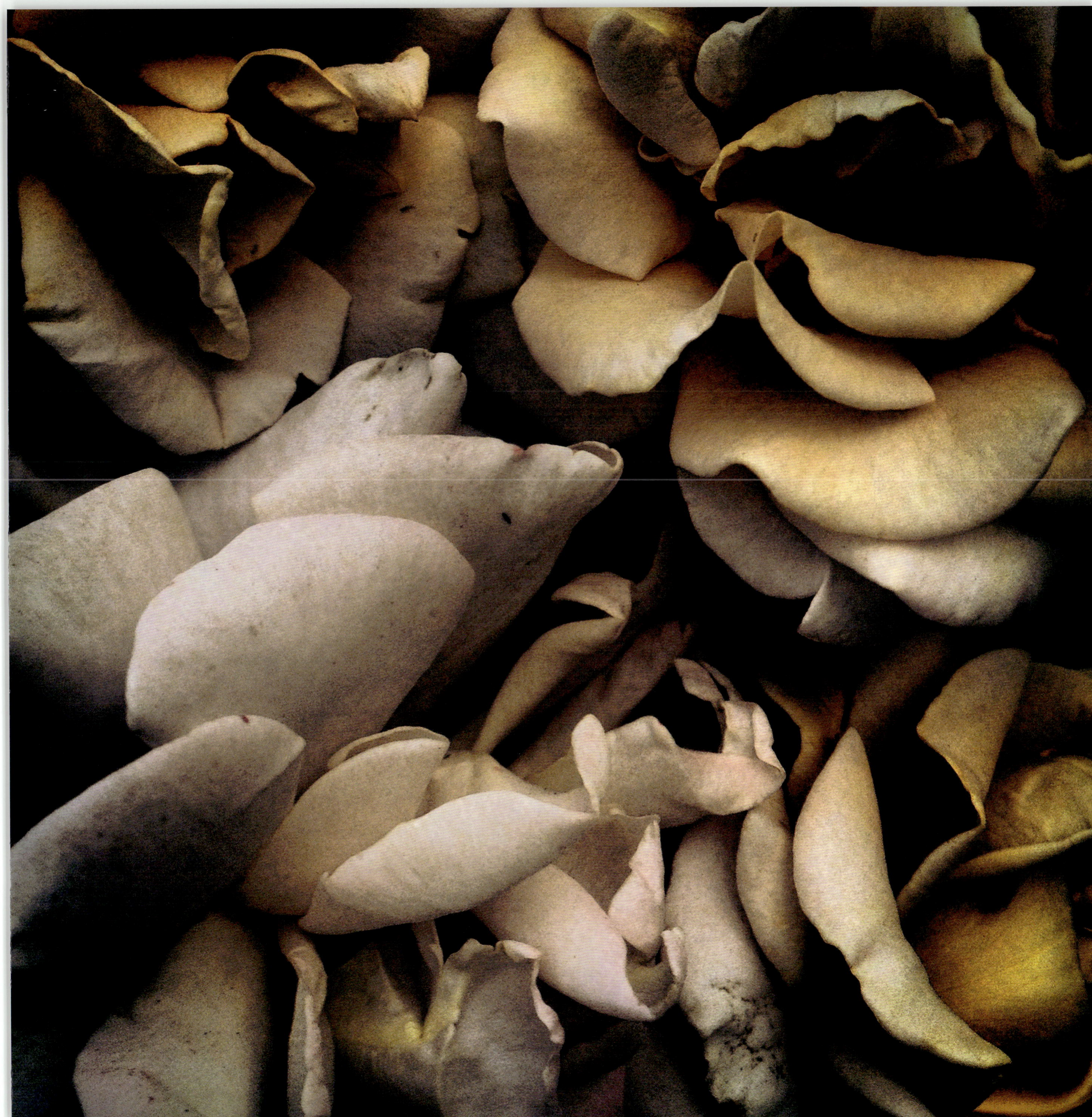

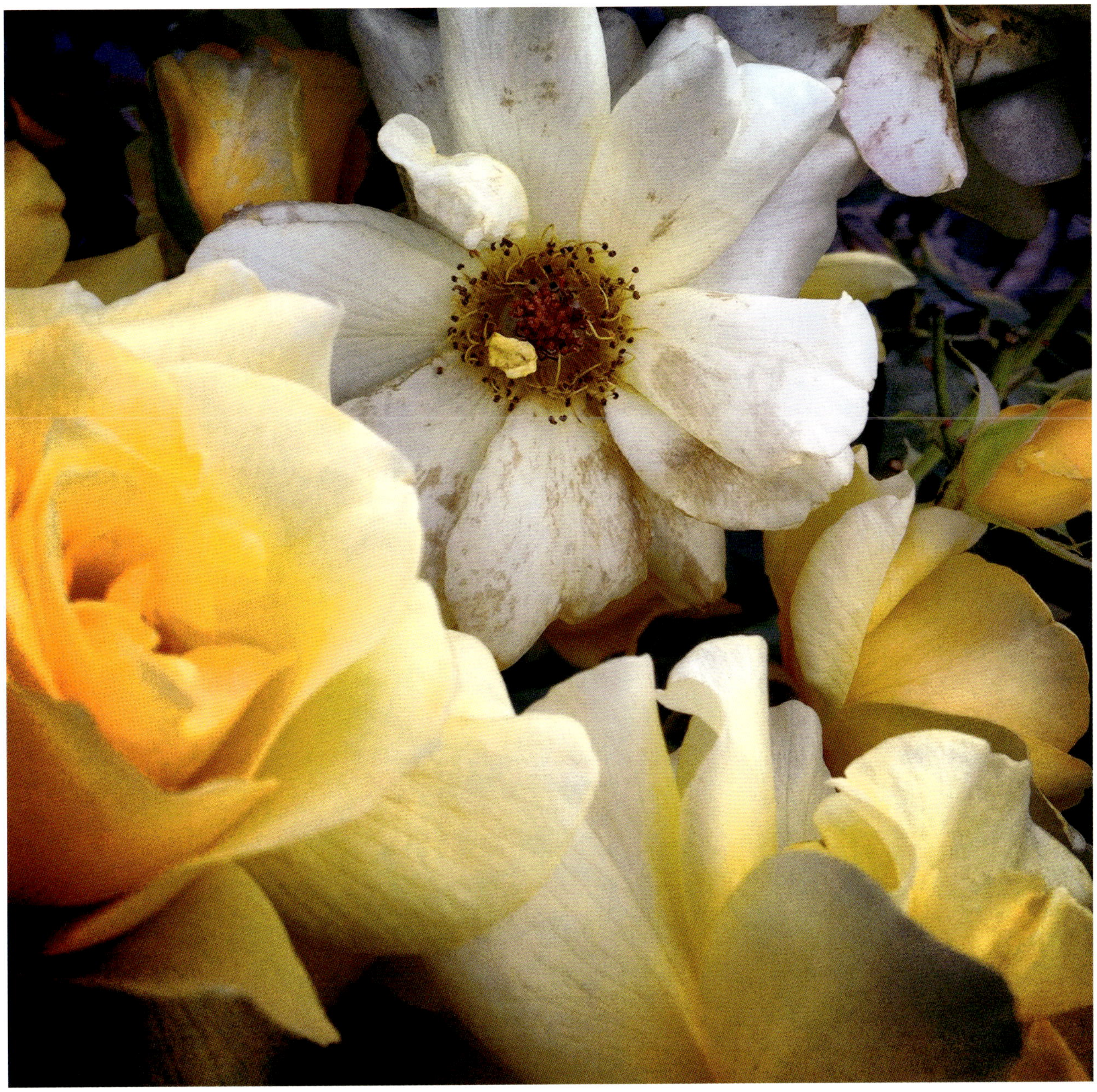

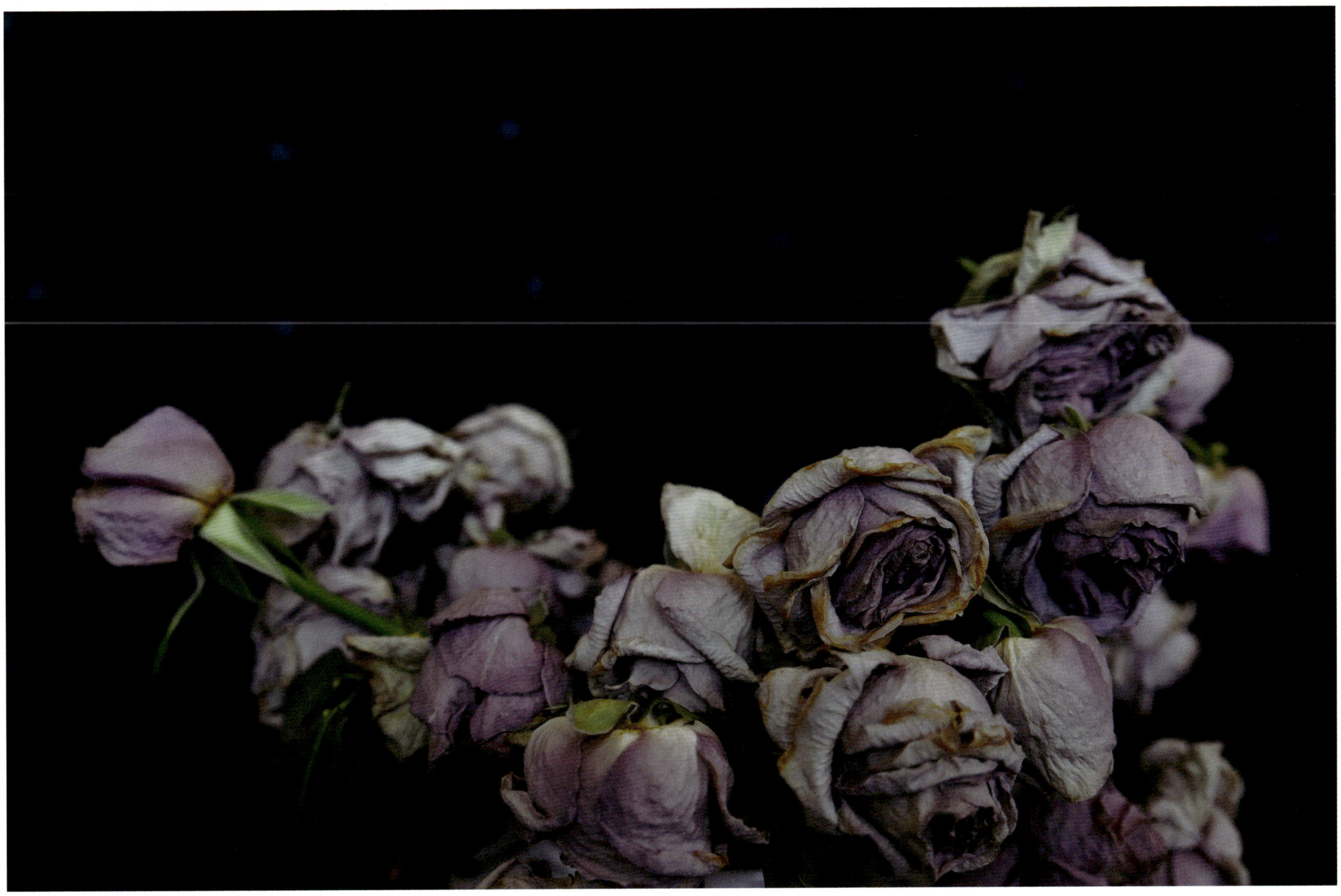

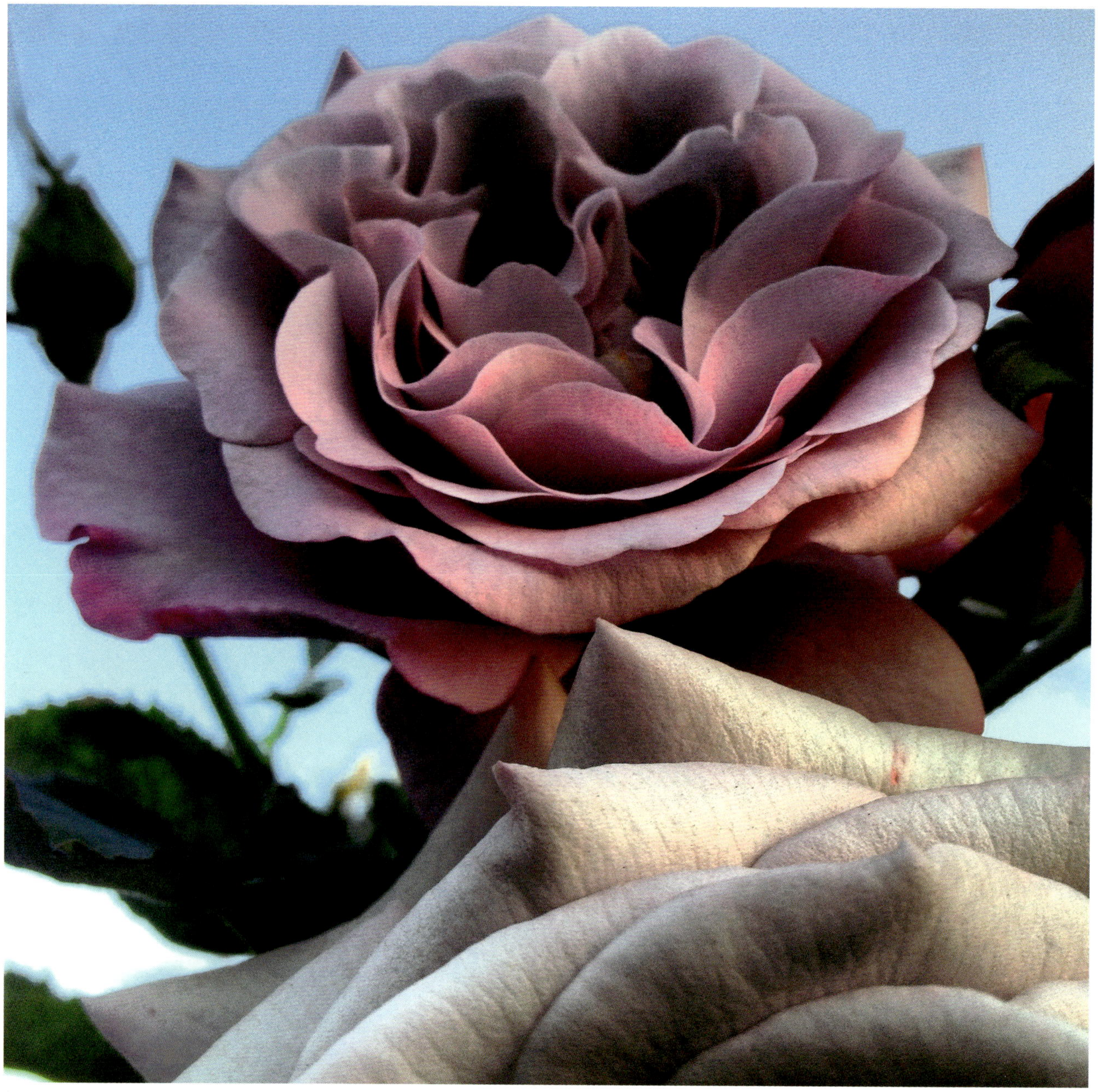

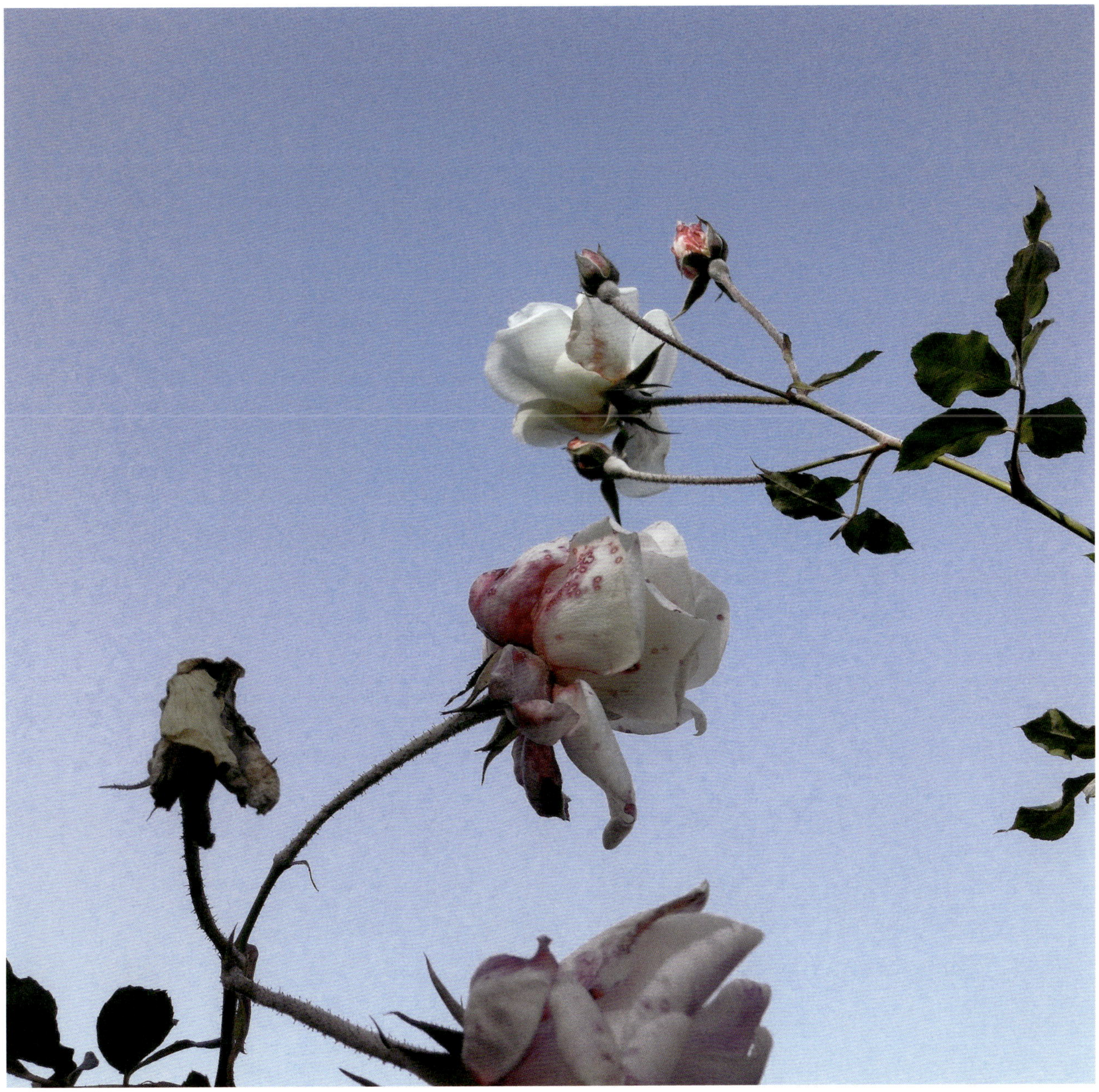

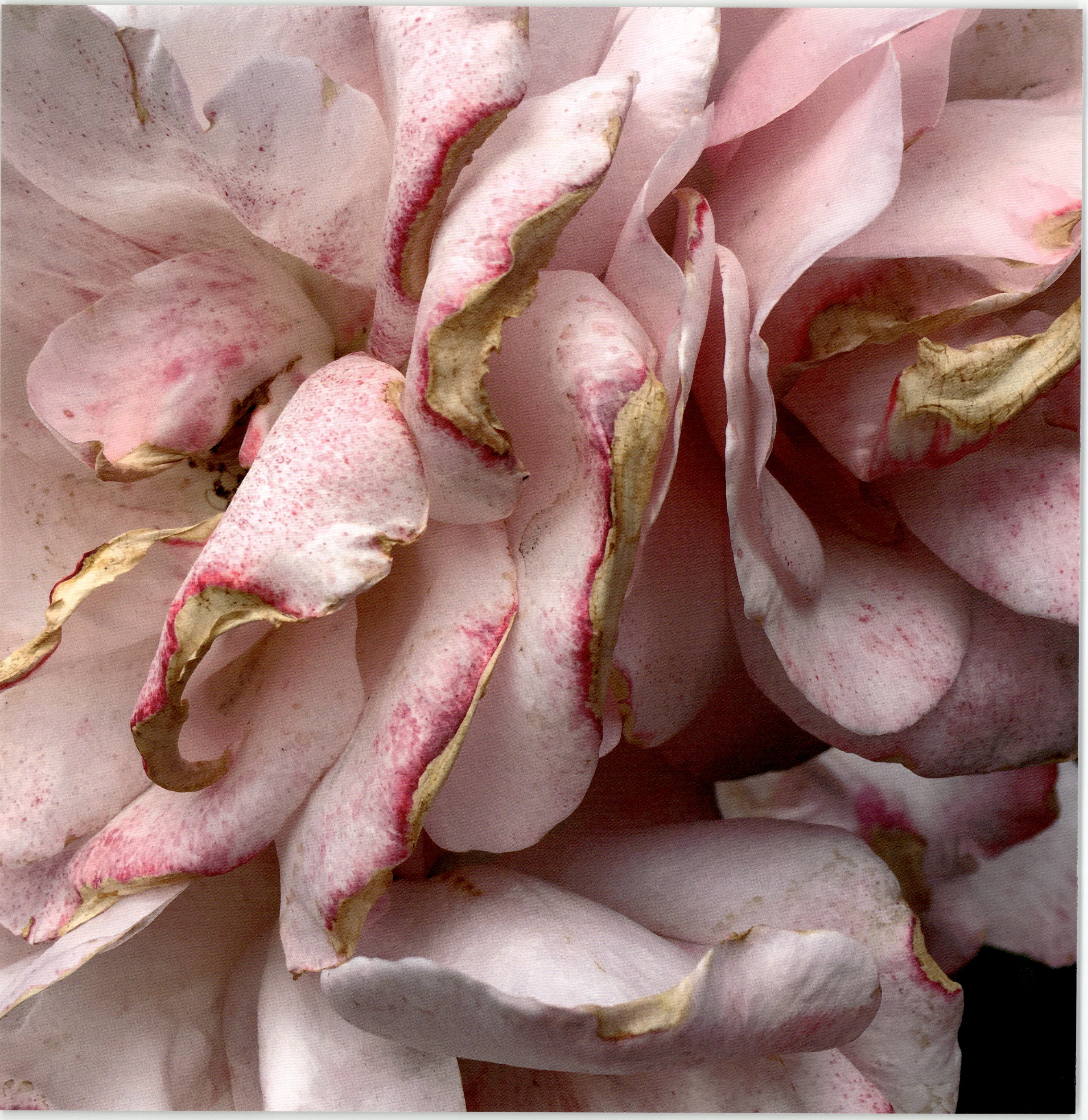

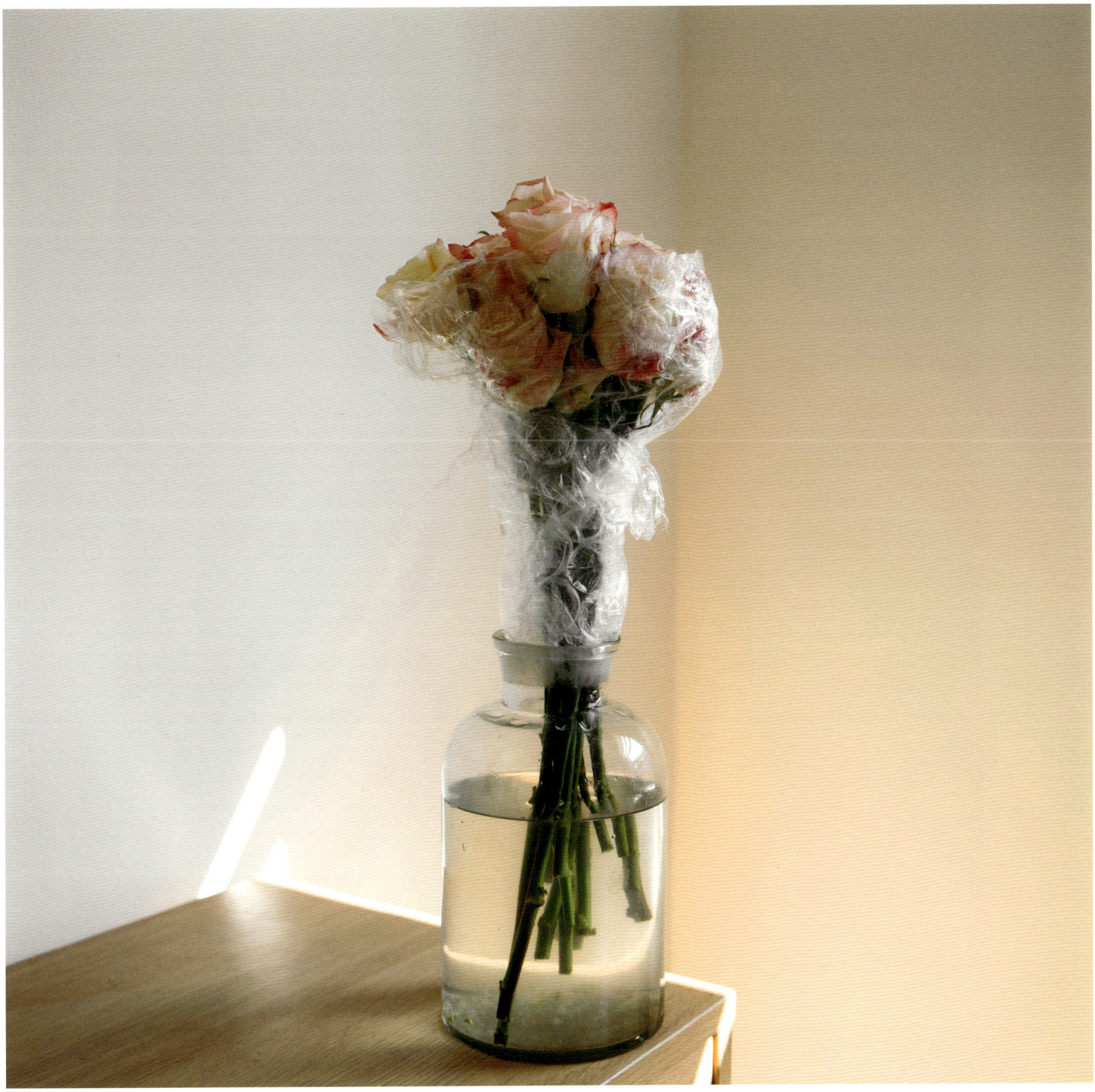

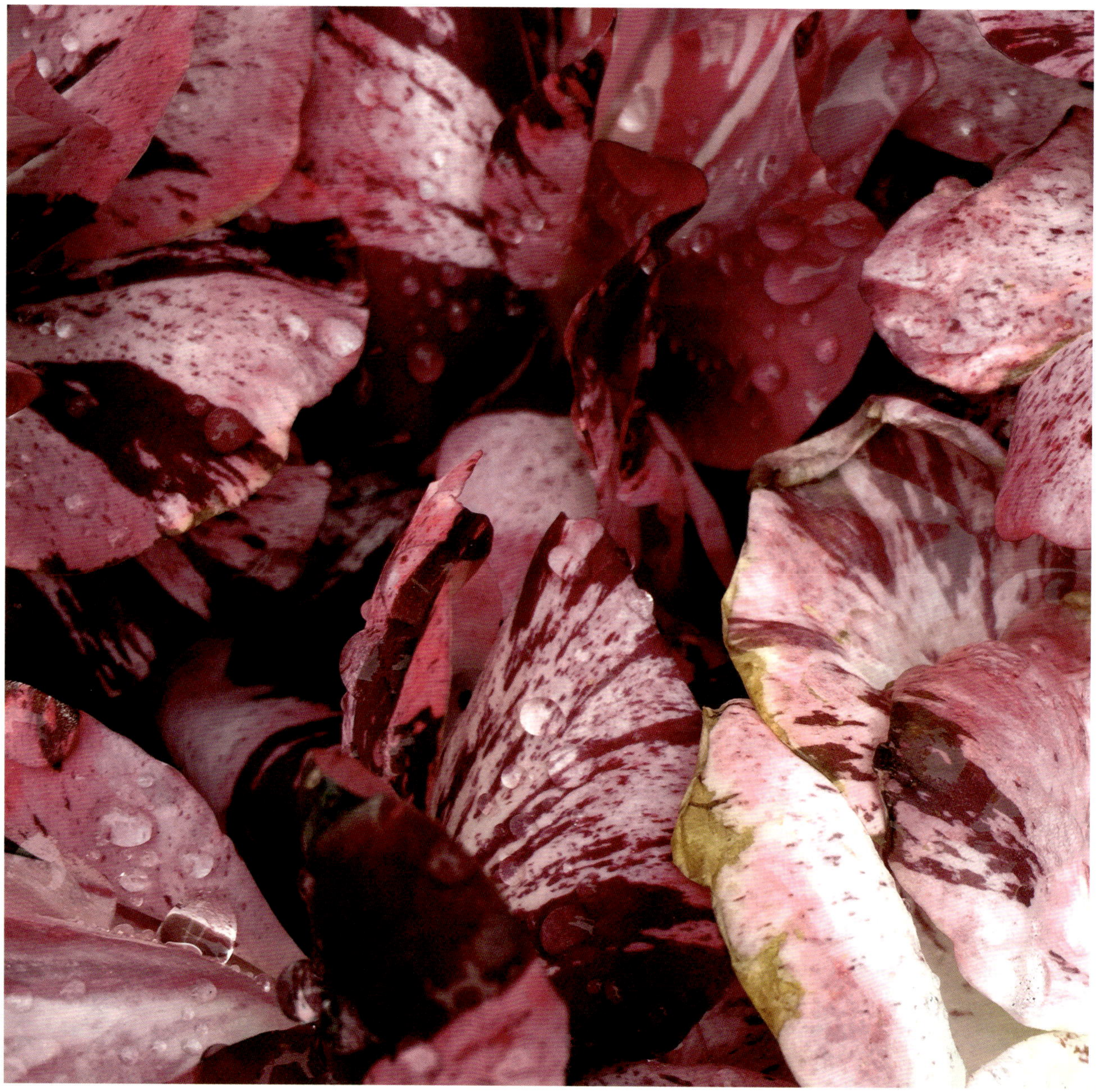

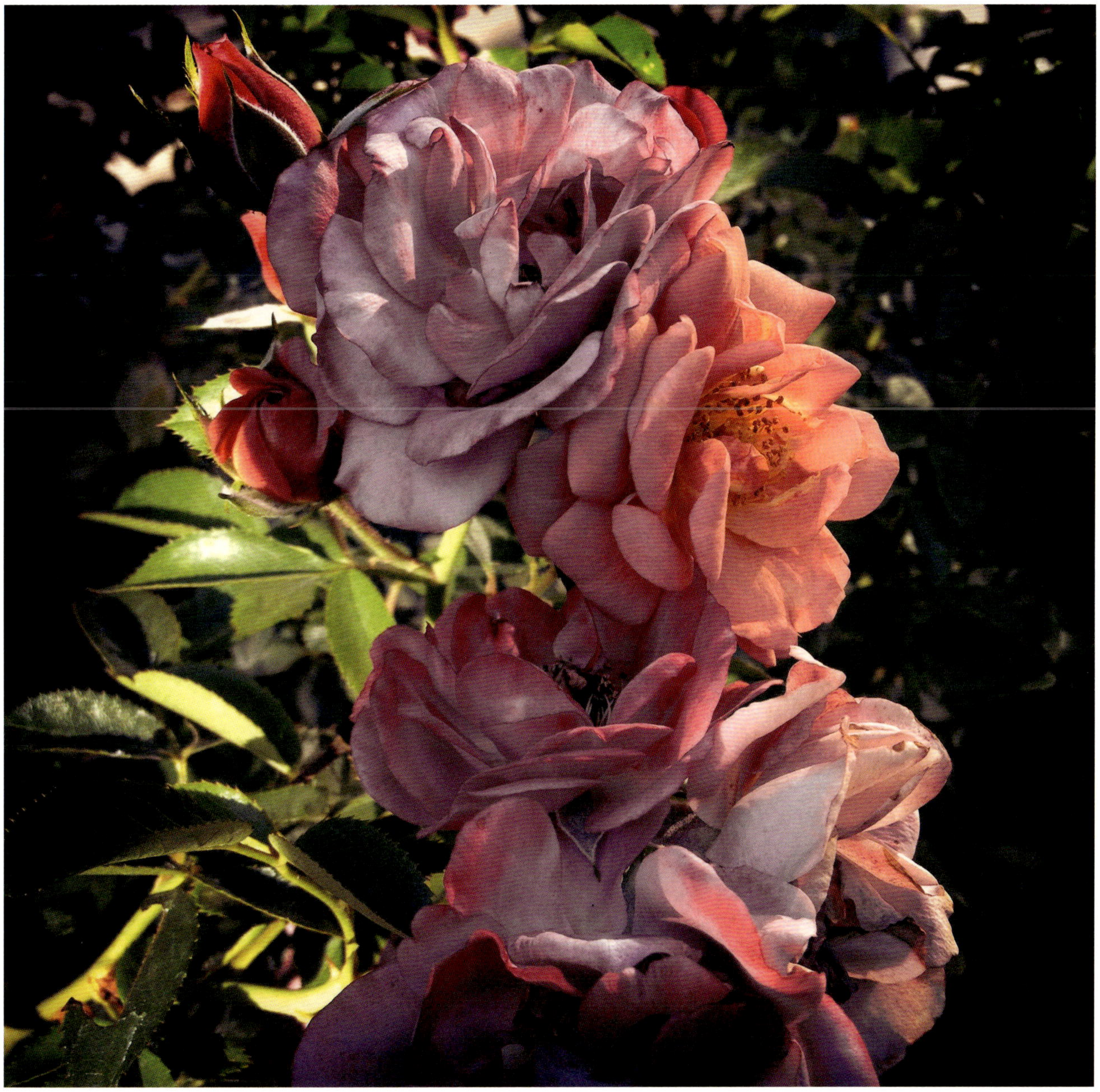

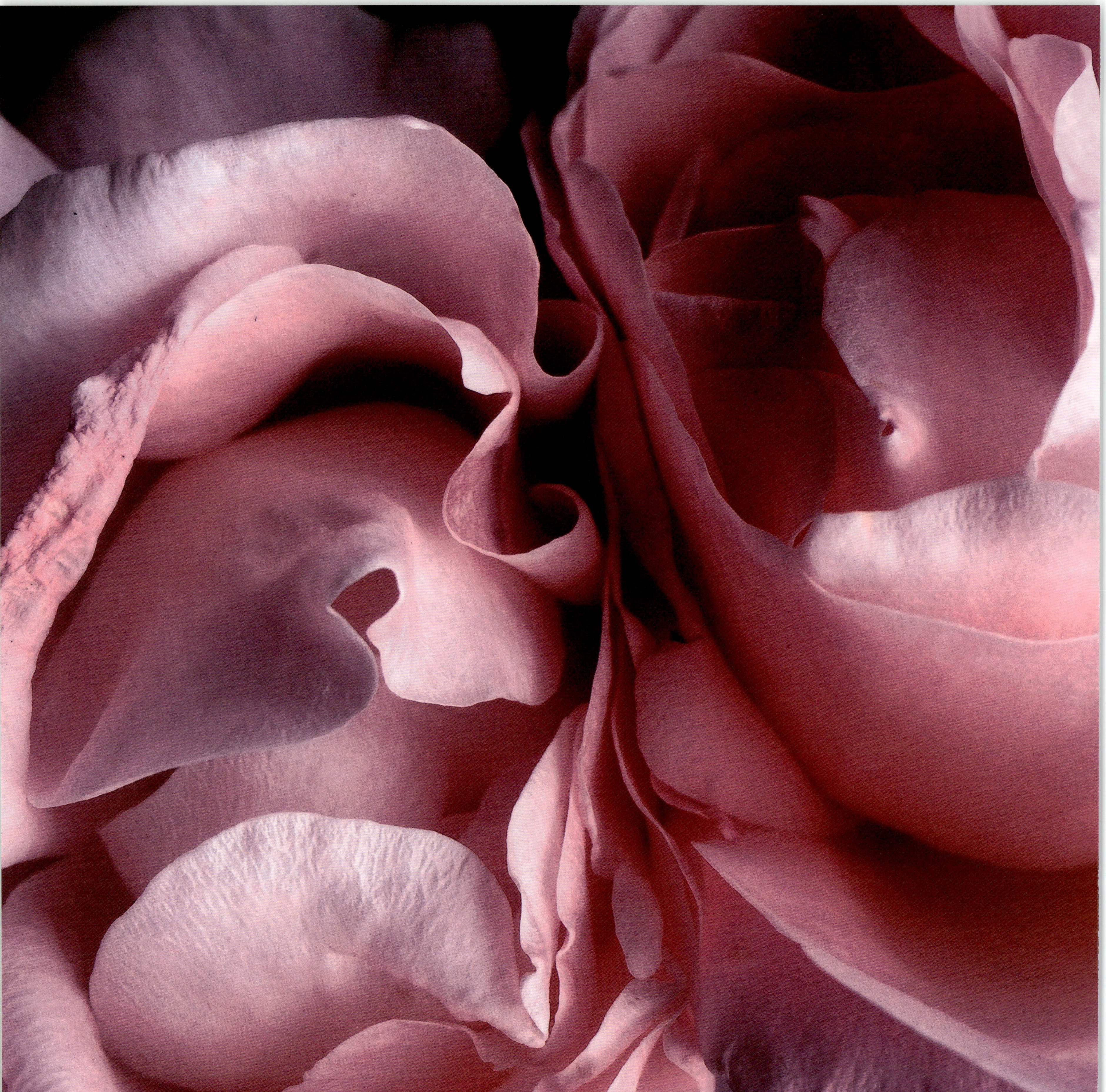

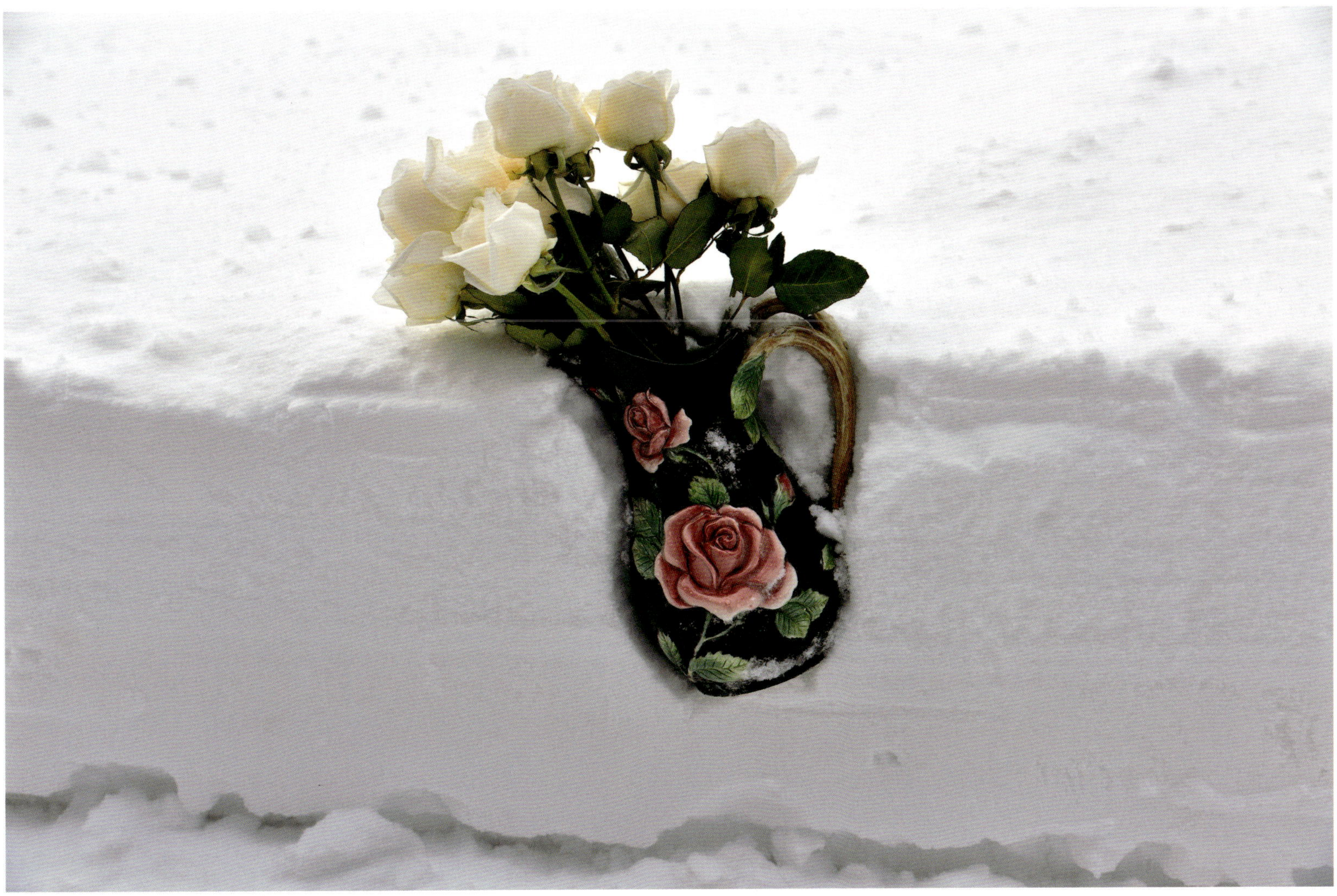

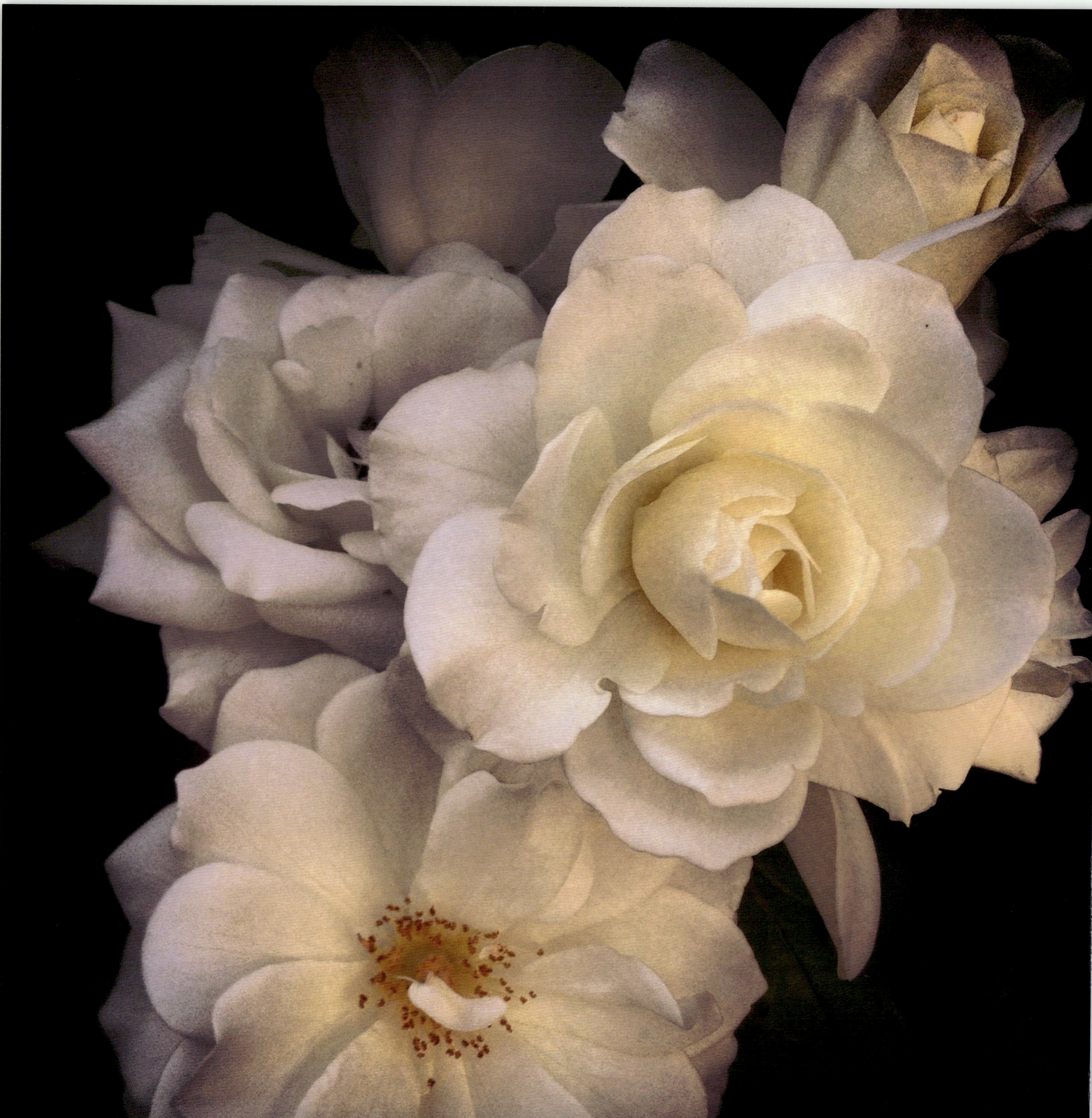

ACKNOWLEDGMENTS

This book would not have been possible without the generous patronage of Lori Uddenberg—I'm forever grateful.

Many thanks to Taj Forer, Michael Itkoff, the team at Daylight Books, Jon San Nicolas, Rock Hushka, Brian Clamp, Cary Stevens, and Buddy Green.

Heartfelt thanks to my husband, Raf, my grandmother Elizabeth, Aunt Kathy, Aunt Meme, Ramine Hajipour, Andy Salzer, Adrian Gilliland, Johnny Ruggiero, Patty Suarez, Jake Berkowitz, Howard Green, Cindy Mena, Michael Moynahan, Floyd Miller, Allison Heutsche, Tracy Tucker Knox, Bonny Taylor, and Paul Batoon.

Special thank you to my family and friends for continuous support and love. xx

ENDNOTES

For You! Modern Day Love Letters: John Arsenault Sub Rosa

[1] This essay is a revised version of the essay originally written for the exhibition *For You!* at the University of Puget Sound, Tacoma, Washington, March 10 to April 12, 2014.

[2] See John Arsenault: *Barmaid* (Daylight Books, 2015).

[3] The iPhone coupled with social media networks has generated a cultural shift back toward one's own self. The ubiquity and possibilities of monetization, not to mention cultivation, of a personal brand, would be, as an example, the publication of Kim Kardashian's *Selfish* (New York, London, Paris, Milan: Rizzoli International, 2015).

[4] J. Ramsbottom, *A Book of Roses With Sixteen Colour Plates after the originals in Redouté's Roses* (Harmondsworth, England: The King Penguin Books, 1939, reprinted 1941), p. 12. It is noteworthy that specialists still recall this rather obscure Greek mythology. Citing an article from the Charleston Lowcountry Rose Society newsletter by Rosalinda Morgan, it was repeated recently in a local newspaper, "Legend has it that Cupid gave a red rose to Harpocrates," *Moultrie News*, February 15, 2014. http://www.moultrienews.com/article/20140216/MN04/140219895/1160/MN/legend-has-it-that-cupid-gave-a-red-rose-to-harpocrates-the-god-of-silence. Accessed March 3, 2014.

LIST OF PLATES

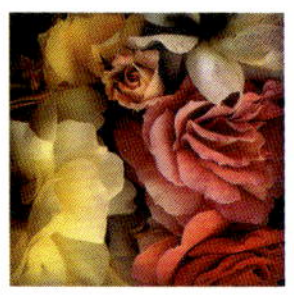

p. 3
3:12 pm
LOS ANGELES, CALIFORNIA, 2013

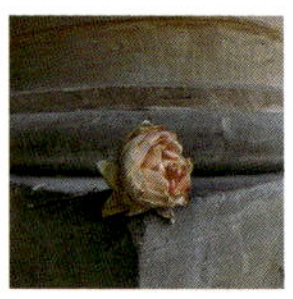

p. 9
3:21 pm
PARIS, FRANCE, 2017

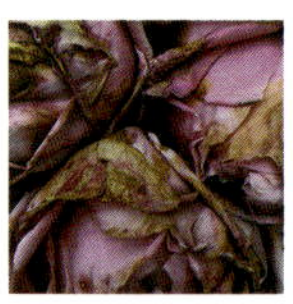

p. 10
11:28 am
PARIS, FRANCE, 2014

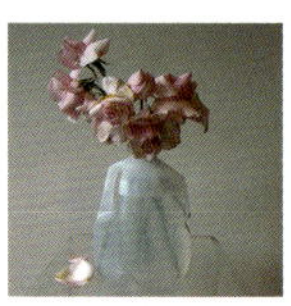

p. 11
10:06 am
BROOKLYN, NEW YORK, 2016

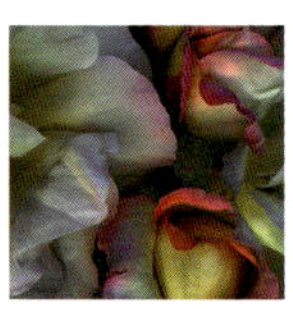

p. 12
6:36 pm
LOS ANGELES, CALIFORNIA, 2014

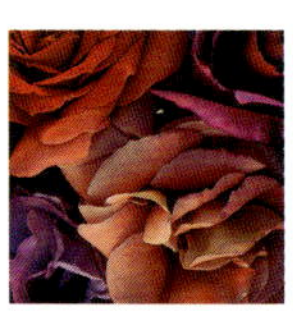

p. 13
1:07 pm
LOS ANGELES, CALIFORNIA, 2013

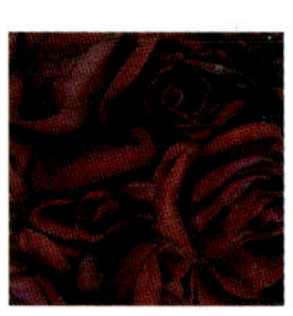

p. 15
6:37 pm
LOS ANGELES, CALIFORNIA, 2016

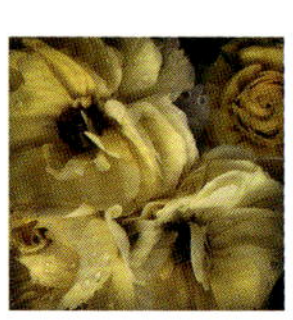

p. 17
1:44 pm
LOS ANGELES, CALIFORNIA, 2014

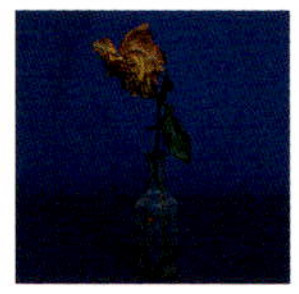

p. 19
6:09 pm
LOS ANGELES, CALIFORNIA, 2016

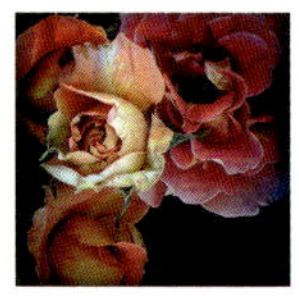

p. 20
7:59 pm
LOS ANGELES, CALIFORNIA, 2013

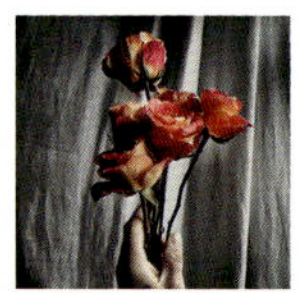

p. 21
4:20 pm
LOS ANGELES, CALIFORNIA, 2013

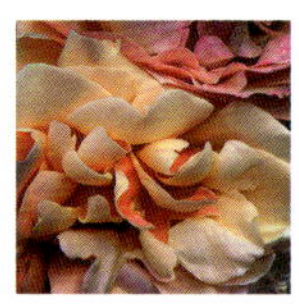

p. 23
1:22 pm
LOS ANGELES, CALIFORNIA, 2014

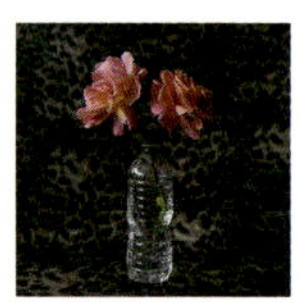

p. 25
12:21 pm
BROOKLYN, NEW YORK, 2016

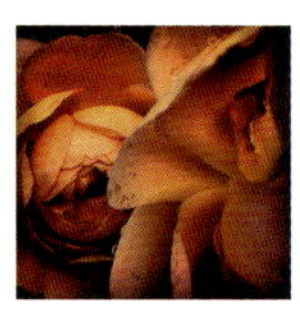

p. 26
1:35 pm
LOS ANGELES, CALIFORNIA, 2013

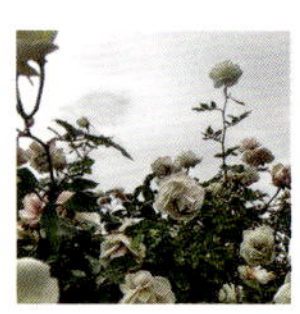

p. 28
5:34 pm
LOS ANGELES, CALIFORNIA, 2013

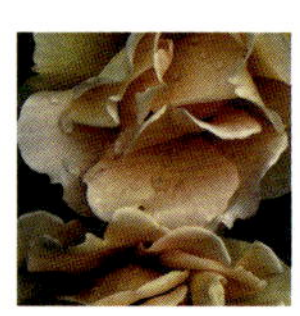

p. 29
5:31 pm
LOS ANGELES, CALIFORNIA, 2013

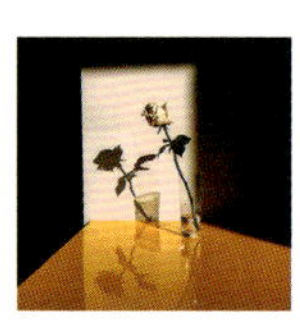

p. 31
5:47 pm
LOS ANGELES, CALIFORNIA, 2016

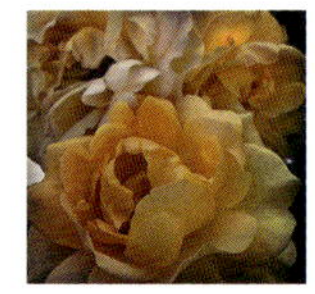

p. 32
8:26 pm
LOS ANGELES, CALIFORNIA, 2013

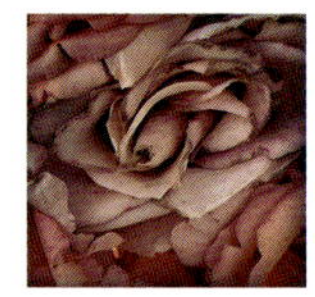

p. 33
4:26 pm
LOS ANGELES, CALIFORNIA, 2014

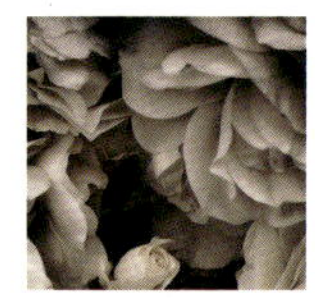

p. 35
11:52 am
LOS ANGELES, CALIFORNIA, 2013

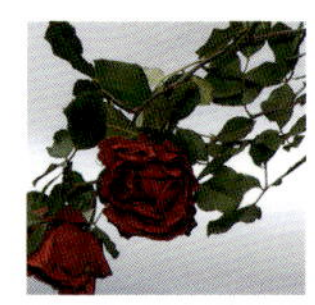

p. 37
11:32 am
BROOKLYN, NEW YORK, 2016

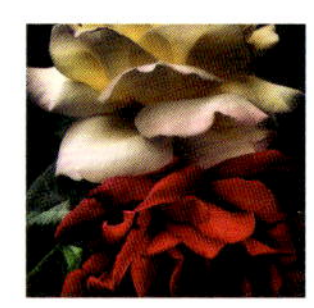

p. 39
11:39 am
LOS ANGELES, CALIFORNIA, 2013

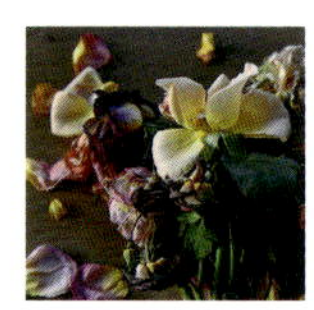

p. 41
11:04 am
LOS ANGELES, CALIFORNIA, 2016

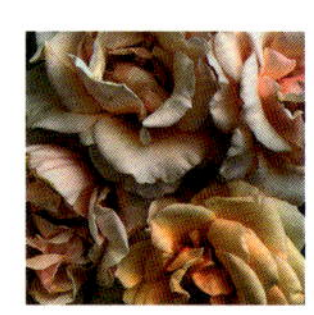

p. 42
8:36 am
LOS ANGELES, CALIFORNIA, 2015

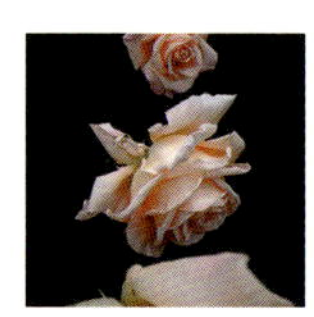

p. 43
1:18 pm
LOS ANGELES, CALIFORNIA, 2013

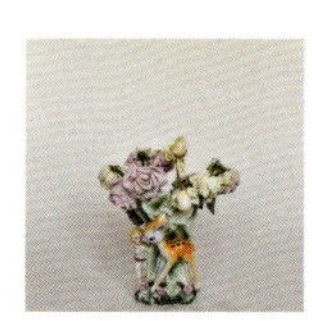

p. 45
7:01 pm
LOS ANGELES, CALIFORNIA, 2016

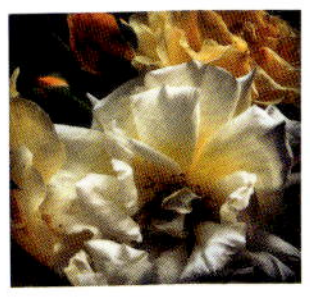

p. 46
3:34 pm
LOS ANGELES, CALIFORNIA, 2013

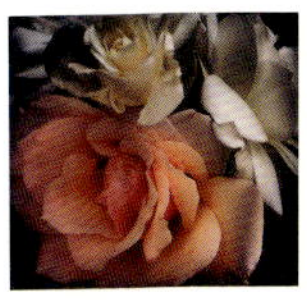

p. 49
5:15 pm
LOS ANGELES, CALIFORNIA, 2013

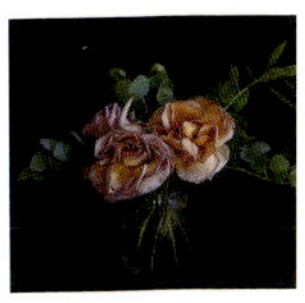

p. 51
12:20 pm
BROOKLYN, NEW YORK, 2016

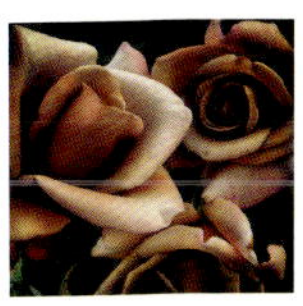

p. 52
5:47 pm
LOS ANGELES, CALIFORNIA, 2013

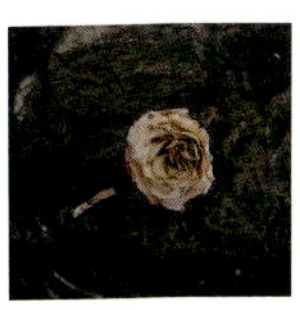

p. 53
6:34 pm
LOS ANGELES, CALIFORNIA, 2016

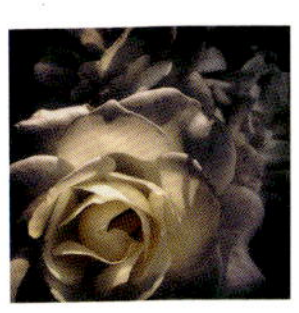

p. 55
11:56 am
LOS ANGELES, CALIFORNIA, 2013

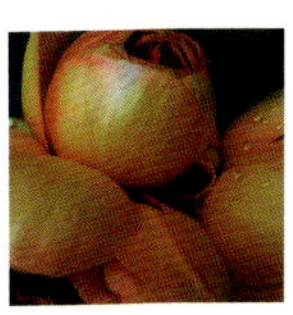

p. 56
11:03 am
LOS ANGELES, CALIFORNIA, 2014

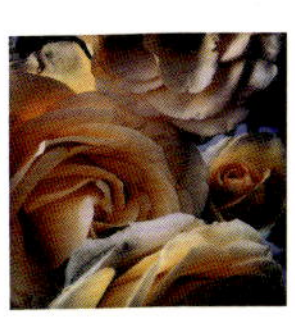

p. 58
4:29 pm
LOS ANGELES, CALIFORNIA, 2013

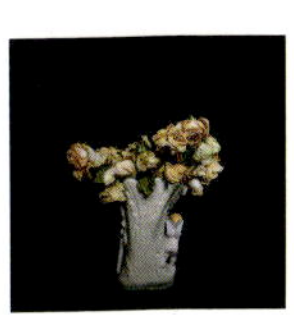

p. 59
8:41 pm
LOS ANGELES, CALIFORNIA, 2016

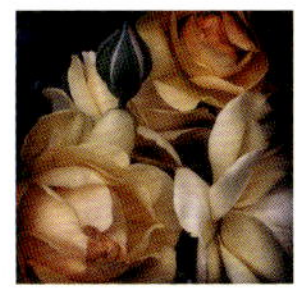

p. 61
4:36 pm
LOS ANGELES, CALIFORNIA, 2013

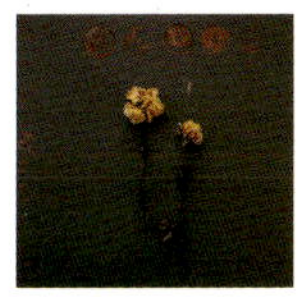

p. 63
6:50 pm
LOS ANGELES, CALIFORNIA, 2016

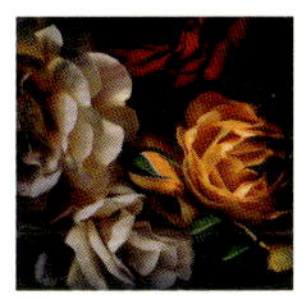

p. 64
5:22 pm
LOS ANGELES, CALIFORNIA, 2013

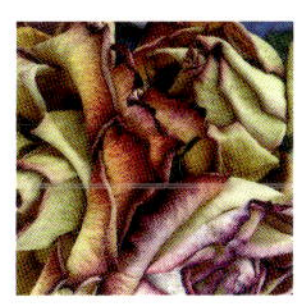

p. 66
11:48 am
LOS ANGELES, CALIFORNIA, 2015

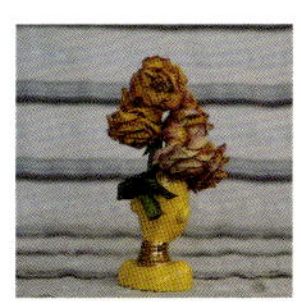

p. 67
5:38 pm
LOS ANGELES, CALIFORNIA, 2016

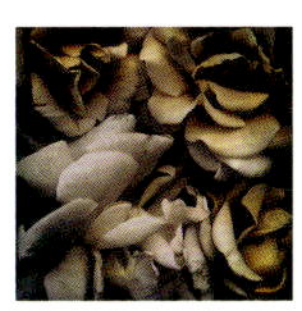

p. 69
12:28 pm
LOS ANGELES, CALIFORNIA, 2013

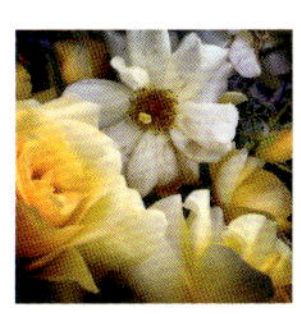

p. 71
2:49 pm
LOS ANGELES, CALIFORNIA, 2012

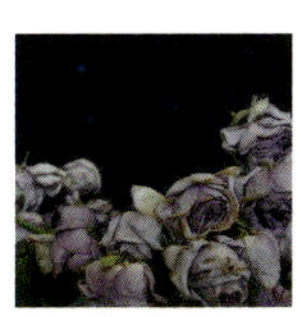

p. 73
5:17 pm
LOS ANGELES, CALIFORNIA, 2016

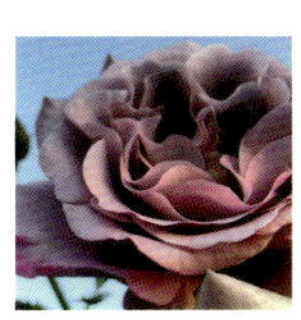

p. 74
7:30 pm
LOS ANGELES, CALIFORNIA, 2013

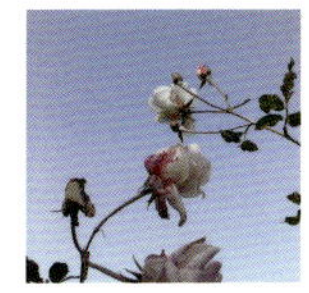

p. 75
6:46 pm
LOS ANGELES, CALIFORNIA, 2013

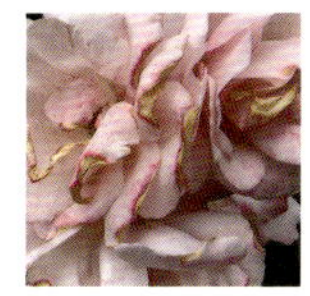

p. 76
11:44 am
LOS ANGELES, CALIFORNIA, 2016

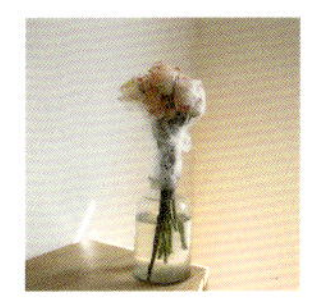

p. 77
10:56 am
BROOKLYN, NEW YORK, 2016

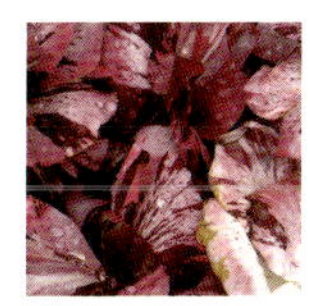

p. 78
9:29 am
LOS ANGELES, CALIFORNIA, 2016

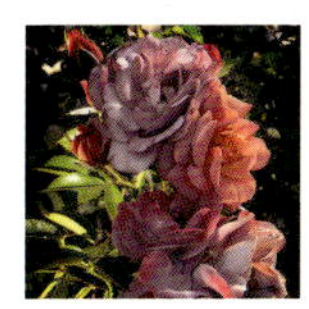

p. 79
5:12 pm
LOS ANGELES, CALIFORNIA, 2012

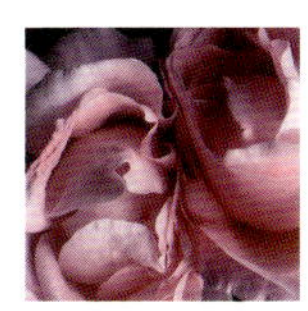

p. 80
12:58 pm
LOS ANGELES, CALIFORNIA, 2014

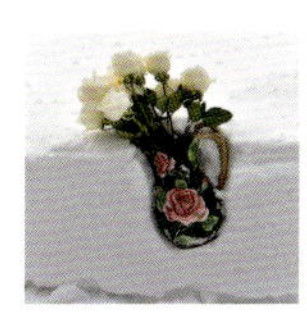

p. 81
9:15 am
HAVERHILL, MASSACHUSETTS, 2017

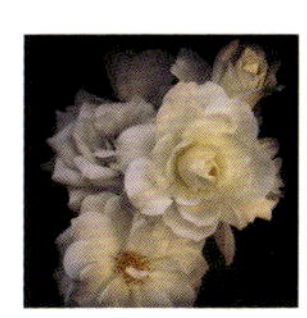

p. 82
9:21 pm
LOS ANGELES, CALIFORNIA, 2013

John Arsenault (b. 1971) was raised in a small town in northern Massachusetts, and he moved to New York City in 1997 to pursue a degree in photography at the School of Visual Arts. He has exhibited five solo shows at ClampArt Gallery in NYC as well as numerous shows across the country and internationally. His first monograph, *Barmaid* (Daylight, 2015), was comprised of portraits, self-portraits, and interior landscapes photographed at the Eagle in Los Angeles. Arsenault's photographs are represented in the permanent collections of the Nerman Museum of Contemporary Art in Overland Park, Kansas; The Museum of Fine Arts in Houston; and the Leslie Lohman Museum of Gay and Lesbian Art in New York City.